SM

I

PRAISE FOR 80/20 BRAND

"Success in any endeavor comes from focusing on what's most important, and 80/20 Brand drives that home. If you're just starting your career in brand building, Hackett's book is your secret guide to a faster start. Or if you're someone that's been at it for a while already, it's a true and practical reminder of what you've often had to learn the hard way. I wish I had this book 20 years ago!"

- ERIC CHRISTIANSON, Former CMO of Perdue Farms

"This book will challenge anyone who really wants to understand brand-building. 80/20 Brand goes directly at the most essential point for a marketer - how to tackle key choices to actually build a brand. Hackett takes a complex topic and turns it into basic principles and lessons in a straightforward delivery."

- TOM PENNER, CEO of Professional Plumbing Group

"Aaron Hackett has written an engaging book that authentically captures the marketing lessons and truisms inherent to the P&G marketing experience. But this book is not just a memory jolt for ex-P&Gers, rather it shares the core tenets to help any marketer on any brand anywhere. One piece in particular stood out for me, which I have also focused on as I have built my career after P&G: good writing comes from good thinking - if you can't concisely write what you want to do and why you should do it, then your thinking isn't good enough either. All business plans should be developed and evaluated as such!"

- ANDREW TOWLE, General Partner at Next Gen Nutrition Investment Partners

"A must & relatively quick read if you want to have a primer on Brand Management 101. Aaron Hackett brings to life the importance of identifying your target to create an engaging Marketing plan for business & brand building. Principles taught in simple concepts of targeting, points of difference, awareness and engagement that will drive delight at the first and second moments of a consumer's brand discovery and use. In a world where brands get seconds to drive engagement, this is a great storytelling led way to inspire brand builders for use across digital and all mediums."

- DAWN W. THOMPSON, Executive Vice President and Head of Brand Management at Hollywood Beauty Products and Former Procter & Gamble Senior Brand Director

"80/20 Brand: Brand Building with a P&G Edge is a must read for all young Brand Builders and entrepreneurs. Aaron does a great job of taking a comprehensive framework for building a brand and condensing it down into simple, usable concepts. Marketers need to better understand brand building and this book provides a great overview. Again, I believe this is a must read."

- GARY DE JESUS, Chief Brand Officer at BRAND'M

"An enjoyable read. This book took me down memory lane, reinforcing actionable principles that should be part of a team's everyday approach. It brings to life new perspectives of marketing in "today's world." Consumer understanding, data analysis, and great storytelling are timeless branding staples. No question that aspiring brand builders will be positively impacted by this book!"

- KERRI CHRISTIAN, Vice President of Marketing at FOCUS Brands

Brand Building
with a
P & G Edge

AARON HACKETT

Notice of Non-Affiliation and Disclaimer
80/20 Brand is not affiliated, associated, authorized, endorsed by, or in any way officially connected with the Procter & Gamble, or any of its subsidiaries or its affiliates beyond the past work experience of the author. The Procter & Gamble website can be found at https://pg.com.

The names P&G, Procter & Gamble, and The Procter & Gamble Company, as well as related names, marks, emblems and images are registered trade-marks of their respective owners.

The information provided in 80/20 Brand: Brand Building with a P&G Edge is provided for informational purposes only. The materials are general in nature; they are not offered as advice on a particular matter and should not be relied on as such. Use of this book does not constitute a legal contract or consulting relationship between 80/20 Brand and any person or entity.

While we make every effort to ensure that the material in this book was accurate and up-to-date when we published it, you should exercise your own independent skill and judgment before you rely on it. In any important matter, you should seek professional advice relevant to your own circumstances. Your use of this book does NOT mean you have received such professional advice.

We take no responsibility for any outcomes to you or your business that you believe may have been influenced by information you read in this book. You retain full responsibility for making your own business judgments and 80/20 Brand in no way warrants any relevance, usefulness or applicability of information on (or provided through) this book to your business activities.

DEDICATION

To my loving wife, Ingrid. You bring the best out of me.

To my inquisitive children, Nadia, Naomi, and Aaron. Being a father to you is among my greatest privileges.

To the motivated Georgia Tech students who take my class. You are the inspiration behind this book.

CONTENTS

INTRODUCTION Stanford versus Procter & Gamble   1

ONE We've got it Backward   10

TWO Consumer is Boss   26

THREE Less is More   39

FOUR Marketers Lie, But Numbers Don't   52

FIVE Opportunity from Chaos   62

SIX Sell a Little, Learn a Lot   81

SEVEN First Moment of Truth   93

EIGHT Product Placebo   107

EPILOGUE 64/4 Brand   125

NOTES   136

ABOUT THE AUTHOR   145

80 ▷ 20 Brand
SM

INTRODUCTION
STANFORD VERSUS PROCTER & GAMBLE

An Educational Perspective

For many events, roughly 80% of the effects come from 20% of the causes.

\-   *Vilfredo Pareto*

Stanford and Procter & Gamble. Not a common comparison, but each uniquely instrumental in my career transformation. These institutions paved my way from engineering to brand management.

After working in engineering for several years, I was fortunate enough to be accepted into Stanford's Graduate School of Business to pursue a Master of Business Administration. This was my dream school, and it exceeded my expectations in every way. Every classmate seemed impressive in his or her own right, and many made significant business contributions quickly after graduation. I was exposed to challenging perspectives, counterintuitive insights, and compelling arguments. There were hours of reading in preparation for each class, but no matter how prepared I was, I felt like I needed to work harder. It was by far my most intellectually stimulating experience.

For my internship, I was offered an assistant brand manager opportunity at The Procter & Gamble Company. Procter & Gamble was considered the brand management powerhouse, but that was not what attracted me. It was Procter & Gamble's reputation as a training ground. I repeatedly heard during my previous visit that there was no better place to learn how to run a business. During my internship on the *Luvs* diaper brand, I experienced what I heard. It was an organization with the structure, rigor, and resources to make most managers successful. At Stanford, I witnessed individual genius. At Procter & Gamble, I saw organizational genius.

A crucial insight I gained from the internship was that brand management was a lot like engineering. I went into engineering because I was a problem solver. Engineering solutions required a thorough understanding of the problem, thoughtful assumptions, and factors of safety when appropriate. Brand managers are also problem solvers, but unlike engineers, their problems do not have a single answer. While engineering problems held to the laws of physics, brand management problems had no such consistency because those problems involved consumers. Consumers do not always act rationally, as economists have come to acknowledge. Brand management was an area of expertise that dealt with problems more complex than those of engineering because of the unpredictability of consumer response.

As graduation from Stanford approached, it was clear that even with a business education that pushed me beyond my perceived limits and deepened my thinking, I needed more than those two years of business education to make a genuine transition from engineering. Many of my classmates went to high tech startups which seemed like a natural transition for a former engineer, but I was not looking for familiar. My Procter & Gamble internship guided me to the right balance. Brand management was grounded in analysis, which gave me a firm foundation. However, there were also psychological and creative elements that were rich areas for professional growth. This combination appeared to be a great way to solidify my business school education. Procter & Gamble was the logical place to continue my business education.

When I arrived as a full-time employee, the training was as advertised. Within the first couple of months, all new brand hires were required to attend the weeklong Assistant Brand Manager College. Monthly, the broader brand teams were invited to training around the latest marketing theories or shared the formulas related to the most prominent internal brand successes. Even the daily brand interactions, such as providing feedback on creative work, were structured in a way to facilitate learning.

At Procter & Gamble, I was in an environment where I learned effortlessly. As I reflect on my growth in the area of brand management, I would summarize Procter & Gamble's success in creating superior brand managers with three components:

- *Application*: We were all actively working on brands and assigned robust work plans. We instinctively vetted everything we learned on our current brands. Nothing was too theoretical because we applied lessons immediately.
- *Structure*: Procter & Gamble is a *promote from within* organization. If a brand manager or marketing director role became available, there was no fear of someone from another company swooping in to take the position. The pool of candidates was set from within the company. This dynamic may be considered incestuous and limiting, but it also created the necessity for superior training. Developing our direct reports

was a core component of our responsibilities. We were evaluated on this skill, just as we were on our business results. Promotion in the organization demanded the ability to develop effective brand leaders.

- *Focus*: I heard about the 80/20 rule at Stanford, but at Procter & Gamble this rule was consistently put into play. Brand managers were swamped. The training P&G offered was helpful because it focused on what mattered most. We codified complex areas of marketing into simple frameworks. Trainers and corporate experts were expected to train in an 80/20 rule fashion. They had to hone in on the 20% of the subject matter that delivered 80% of the results. In this way, brand managers were able to thrive, specifically learning what was essential to build their brands.

It was this emphasis on focus that drove the most significant contrast from Stanford. At Stanford, there was a ton of preparation and divergent conversations that exposed the breadth of each topic. The level of breadth that might prepare a doctoral candidate to consider which area of a particular field to research. At Procter & Gamble, there was no supplemental preparation, and focused efforts went deep into the few concepts we needed to take away and reapply. Busy brand managers demanded to know what could be immediately applied to their brands to make the most significant impact. I cannot lavish enough praise on the Stanford Graduate School of Business experience. However, in one area, Procter & Gamble was superior: brand management training. The beneficial magnitude of an 80/20 approach to brand training would not be apparent to me for more than a decade.

In 2013, I began teaching Strategic Brand Management at the Georgia Institute of Technology Scheller College of Business. I was back in an environment catered to doctoral students attempting to teach what I experienced in practice. In the first semester, I followed the recommended flow used previously along with the prior textbook. We covered fifteen chapters, over 500 pages, of the textbook. The students gave positive class feedback and appeared engaged, but I knew in my gut that this was not the best preparation for what they would experience in the workforce.

Given my professional background, I felt a responsibility to help students sift through the vast information, identify what mattered most, and provide ways to apply these principles effectively. I began pruning the class each semester, dropping from fifteen chapters to six chapters, to ultimately four chapters with the supporting content from my experience. I did not want to spend time on topics that brand managers would not experience until two or three years after starting, if ever. My students needed to hit the ground running. In that 80/20 spirit, the fewer chapters I taught, the higher the student class feedback ratings, and the more letters of appreciation I received from former students working on brands. As I omitted the portions of the texts rarely used in industry, I was able to hone the understanding of the most critical areas of brand management to students in a way that they could easily internalize.

With over five years of teaching Strategic Brand Management at the MBA and undergraduate levels, I had taken the complexities of brand management and reduced them to focused ways of thinking. The glaring exception to this refinement was the book. Students were paying over $200 for a book in which we only covered four chapters, and that led to a test that was, well, by the book. This confused what mattered most.

As the culmination of this teaching journey, it has become my mission to fix what was missing. Students of brand management need what brand managers need. They need a book with fewer terms and more application. They need a book that does not attempt to cover every conceivable situation, but instead a book that will teach them the 20% that is necessary on virtually all brands.

I have worked in many categories and on dozens of brands since my *Luvs* internship in 1998. *80/20*

Brand: Brand Building with a P&G Edge is what brand builders need based on my experiences as a brand leader, a brand consultant, and a brand professor. Teaching this topic in the classroom was particularly enlightening. I was teaching what I was thinking about, but I realized that I did not think about many of my decisions. I had a seasoned gut feel about many aspects of brand management that I never had to explain to direct reports because they also learned from experience. Through student feedback and analysis of their brand project recommendations, I have pinpointed areas that require specific explanation. In the classroom, I was able to identify the gut calls and the rationale behind them.

I firmly believe the 80/20 philosophy of teaching brand management is ideal because over time more of my students have demonstrated a readiness to build brands immediately. Their brand consulting project recommendations are as sharp and as thoughtful as most of the assistant brand managers, and some of the brand managers, I have had the privilege of managing.

On one occasion we had a chance to do a small marketing test between the recommendations of one of my undergraduate groups versus an existing brand. The recommendations of the undergraduate group tripled the results of the current marketing efforts. More details on this opportunistic test will be covered later in the book.

For this book to deliver similar benefits to you, it is essential that you have a brand in mind to build. It could be a brand you are working on, a brand you plan to create, or a brand that is somehow relevant to you. Applying what we learned to our brands at Procter & Gamble was vital. Thinking about how the lessons from this book apply to a specific brand will internalize your learning.

This book does not endeavor to cover the topic of brand management comprehensively. Instead, it reduces the complexity of brand management to its simplest, yet most effective core.

ONE WE'VE GOT
IT BACKWARD

The 80/20 of Targeting

> *The battle is won miraculously by an underdog who, by all expectations, should not have won at all... And the problem with that version of the events is that almost everything about it is wrong.*

> -   *Malcolm Gladwell*

It is a mind-opening experience when we discover that something we have always accepted as true is exposed not to be factually correct, or even the opposite of what we held in our minds for so long. Sometimes we get it backward.

One example is the title story of Malcolm Gladwell's *David and Goliath: Underdogs, Misfits, and the Art of Battling Giants*. In the famous story of David and Goliath, David is a young shepherd boy who volunteers to battle Goliath, a six-foot, nine-inch giant, when no one else will challenge him. Goliath is clad in armor with a mighty sword, while David only has a slingshot. As the story goes, David, with a stroke of luck, strikes Goliath right between the eyes with a stone from his slingshot and gains an improbable victory over the mighty giant. This story exemplifies our desire to root for the underdog.

According to Gladwell's research, this firmly held understanding is backward. David was not the underdog. No, he was the heavy favorite. First, the slingshot he used was not the childhood variety we find in toy stores. An artillery unit of armies, called slingers, used them in battle. These slingers were noted to be accurate from a distance of 200 yards. David sharpened his slinging skills defending his flock from predators and was much closer to Goliath than 200 yards. The sling structure combined with the dense stones in the area of battle gave David stopping power comparable to a 45mm handgun. Slingers were often the decisive factor in victories versus infantry.

Goliath enters the matchup with a misunderstanding of the rules of engagement. He expects to engage in hand-to-hand combat where size is an advantage. Instead, he was the target of projectiles. In this situation size was a disadvantage. To compound Goliath's bleak situation, he is speculated to have suffered from acromegaly, one of the most common causes of gigantism. The extreme height is noted to frequently come with a range of symptoms and complications, including limited joint mobility and impaired vision. Looking back at it, Goliath brought a knife to a gunfight. Poor guy did not have a chance.

Our marketing efforts may not have a chance either if we do not correctly apply key marketing concepts. Some of the most salient concepts we take for granted, impatiently skimming over them. Although this is true for more than one marketing concept, in my experience with marketing clients and college students one concept is misunderstood and misapplied significantly more than others.

Targeting is one of the most fundamental marketing concepts. It indeed is a strategic decision that will drive essential choices throughout the marketing program. Unfortunately, many marketers are getting it backward although with good intentions.

Precise targeting has a perceived drawback. When the business *goal* is to maximize revenue, intuition leads us to sell to as many people as possible. To sell to as many people as possible, we need to make compromises in our products or services. We need to be generally appealing and avoid catering to the specific needs of any particular subgroup. Our messaging must be careful to make everyone comfortable rather than leverage a unique insight that would emotionally connect with a critical consumer subset while potentially turning off another subset. The broader the target, the greater the compromise. We end up with a brand that many people like, but no one loves. To build a meaningful brand, we need consumers to love it.

In class, I ask students the following question. Assuming you are in a category that has the specific appeal (see Chart 1 below) with five strategic targets about equal size, which brand would you prefer to manage? Everyone likes brand A. No one loves it, but no one hates it. One target (20%) loves Brand B, but the other four targets (80%) hate it.

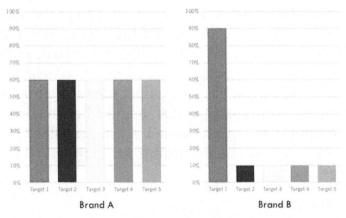

Chart 1: Target appeal for Brand A and Brand B

Instinctively, the majority of the class chooses Brand B, benefitting from targeting lessons of previous marketing classes. A couple of students usually still push for Brand A emphasizing the natural appeal of more customers. After we leave this theoretical example and begin working with actual brands, the majority of the class subtly switches from preferring targeting like Brand B for the more intuitive targeting of Brand A.

Of course, the better brand depends on circumstances. In the overwhelming number of situations, Brand B is the better option, although Brand A is preferable in specific cases. For example, in a monopoly Brand A wins gaining the business of four of the strategic targets. However, few categories have monopolies or only a couple of brands.

Look at a scenario that could develop as the category expands to merely six brands (see Chart 2 below.) Brand A still has the broadest appeal, with the other five brands only appealing to a single strategic target, but each target now has a brand it loves more than Brand A. Brand A becomes the compromise option. Brand A can get sales this way, but it is not positioned for long-term success.

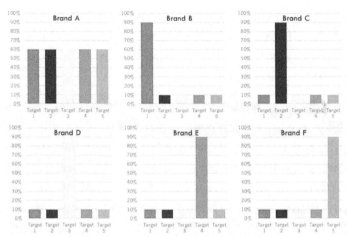

Chart 2: Target appeal as the category grows

Having a lot of consumers is great. It is more important to have passionate consumers. You get them by being the best in that area. If you are good, but not great, you will still make sales, but most often to those who are not as invested in the category and with those not as likely to tell others of your brand. To understand, you must put yourself in the place of a consumer who cares deeply about a category and is in the purchase decision process. Healthcare is a category that dramatically illustrates this point.

You need a heart transplant. Do you go to the doctor represented by Brand A who is better than average at heart transplants and also better than average in many other areas such as dermatology, gynecology, and oncology, or do you go to the doctor represented by Brand B, who is the best at heart transplants, but with little competence in the other areas? The more important the purchase decision, the more the consumer focuses on what matters most.

If 20% of consumers loving your brand is preferable to 100% liking your brand, how might this play out in the real world? How does a hair weave brand identify the subsegment of consumers most worthy of marketing investment? How does a premium dog food brand understand what behaviors lead to owners who are willing to pay more for their beloved dog? In a category as broadly appealing as teeth whitening, why not go after a broader target such as women 18-39 years of age?

80/20 TARGET

To emphasize the strategic importance of targeting and provide the motivation to exclude potential consumers, I use the term *80/20 target* with my students and clients. In other words, the 20% of consumers who drive 80% of your revenue. In addition to identifying your *80/20 target*, you want to understand this target as intimately as possible.

HAIR WEAVE WINNERS

One of my first significant clients as an independent consultant was a national leader in premium hair extensions. The brand had a defined target of black women. This target selection was for a couple of reasons. First, the brand learned that black women were willing to spend a disproportionate amount of money on hair care. This consumer dynamic was a key component of much of the work I did at Procter & Gamble when I was the brand manager of Multicultural Marketing. The time and money black women spent maintaining beautiful hair were an order of magnitude above that of the general population. The second reason the brand focused on black women, rather than all women, is that the process for installing extensions for black women was unique. Targeting black women seemed to make sense.

As a smaller business, this client did not have a marketing staff. So, I rolled up my sleeves and did much of the marketing work. A particularly enlightening activity was analyzing consumer sales data. On one occasion, I took the annual sales data and sorted consumers based on sales. The consumers were virtually all black women, but I was curious about what I would find.

The 80/20 rule played out again. About 20% of the consumers accounted for 80% of the sales of an already valuable target. I was curious who these consumers were and how we could market to them.

It turns out the top 20% of consumers were hairstylists. They not only used the hair themselves but resold the hair units to their customers. This insight encouraged us to focus our marketing efforts. We created a Recommended Hairstylists page on our website with names and addresses searchable by proximity. We also offered the ability for hairstylists to purchase private label lines of hair, allowing them to build their shop brands. These high-leverage efforts fueled brand growth by increasing the loyalty of our most valuable target.

This is a classic example of not only a heavy user, but of a gatekeeper: a person who has substantial influence over the brand choices of others. Sunny Delight used the gatekeeper dynamic when marketing how hip and fun its beverage was to kids while communicating vitamin content to moms.

After working through this example, the *80/20 target* for a hair weave brand may seem evident in retrospect. How about a more complicated case?

EXPENSIVE DOG FOOD

For a while, Procter & Gamble was in the pet food business after purchasing *Iams* and *Eukanuba*. *Eukanuba* was a premium brand. At a marketing mixer, I engaged on the topic of targeting with an assistant brand manager from the brand. Like most P&G brands, *Eukanuba* had reams of data and statistical analysis. Given the price point of *Eukanuba*, merely targeting dog owners seemed inefficient.

The most common *80/20 target* guess among students is dog owners with higher incomes. However, like black women in the hair care category, investment was not strongly correlated with income. As students move beyond demographics to psychographics, the next common guess is people who consider the dog to be a member of the family. Although this characteristic is correct, it doesn't help identify the *80/20 target*. When asked, virtually all dog owners consider the pet a part of the family.

The *Eukanuba* brand was able to cleverly create a question to identify a specific behavior that allowed them to identify the brand *80/20 target*. The question is *Do you celebrate your dog's birthday?* This behavior allowed the brand to move from a proclaimed belief which no one would deny (our dog is a family member) to a behavior that demonstrated the extent a loved one would endure for any other family member. Moving from proclaimed beliefs to behaviors sharpens the target focus.

REFINE YOUR 80/20 TARGET ON LAUNCH

Most categories do not have a target as recognizable as hairstylists, and most brands do not have the level of data a company like Procter & Gamble does. If executed correctly, your brand launch can sharpen your target.

Vince Hudson was the brand manager who launched the wildly successful *Crest Whitestrips*; Procter & Gamble's first digital brand. At the time, fellow Procter & Gamble employees described a digital brand as a brand with no retail distribution. Consumers could only purchase the brand online in the first year. Given a price point over twenty dollars combined with a low package weight, a digital-only *Whitestrips* launch was feasible.

As background, most initiatives, even from Procter & Gamble, fail. *Whitestrips* was a great success due in large part to Hudson's commitment to the launch. To unequivocally show the effectiveness of this product, Hudson became a walking demonstration for *Whitestrips*. He used the product on his top teeth only, leaving his bottom teeth as they were. To make his point at sales meetings, he did not have to rely on data or testimonials; he confidently shared the contrast in his smile.

Hudson's commitment to success extended to his launch strategy. At a conference away from headquarters, Hudson coached me on his plan for precisely understanding his *80/20 target*.

At launch, *Crest Whitestrips* built into its price a five-dollar discount for every package sold. It was this five-dollar discount, along with online-only sales that would develop an incredibly rich *80/20 target*. The marketing plan used many traditional and digital media to build *awareness*. The marketing also included a call to action: discount codes offering the five-dollar discount. Each magazine, radio show, website, podcast, and any other media vehicle had a unique discount code. Therefore, the five-dollar discount was not only a call to action, but it was a conversion metric. By tracking quantities of each discount code used, Hudson was able to determine not only the most efficient marketing spends but use the target of those vehicles to uncover who was buying a disproportionate amount of *Whitestrips*.

When determining the *80/20 target*, it might be natural to identify problem solvers. Problem solvers in this context would be consumers you would expect to have yellower teeth, such as coffee drinkers and smokers. Surprisingly, the most significant return on investment from the marketing effort was from an aspirational consumer segment: brides-to-be. Rather than seeking to cover an issue, many problem solvers most likely had become accustomed to yellower teeth. The most motivated problem solvers presumably went to the dentist or adjusted their habits to address this issue. However, brides-to-be envisioned a perfect day. An incremental investment to enhance a beautiful wedding day image was irresistible.

MULTIPLY RATHER THAN BROADEN

Crest focused disproportionately on brides-to-be but given that *Crest* is a multi-billion-dollar brand, the brand marketing goes well beyond this target. I am not privy to any information on the marketing efforts of *Whitestrips* beyond the launch. A more resource-constrained brand would also invest disproportionately on brides-to-be. This *80/20 target* is a significant target that could maintain a brand's efforts for decades.

What if a company in this space had fewer resources than *Crest*, but believed it saturated the brides-to-be target within this market? This situation might be when a brand would broaden the target and market to married women or women ages 19 to 29, but is this the way to spend your limited marketing dollars?

A more productive way to spend incremental marketing dollars would be to go after a second highly attractive target. A part of the original *Whitestrips* launch learning that I didn't mention earlier, is that there was a second target about as appealing as brides-to-be, and with no overlap. This second target was metrosexuals. Demographically metrosexuals are male, but it is their behavior that sets them apart from most males. Metrosexuals by definition care disproportionately more about their appearance and therefore are meticulous about their grooming and fashion. Both Brides-to-be and Metrosexuals shared a desire to perfect their look. In this business, the aspiration to be better was more motivating than a desire to reduce imperfections like those of coffee drinkers and smokers.

This precise focus on brides-to-be and metrosexuals enables more compelling marketing than a marketing plan with a broader focus meant to meet the needs of a more general audience. Of course, multiple *80/20 targets* require multiple marketing plans. There will be similar insights and tactics, but to speak directly to each target, we need specific marketing plans per target.

Common *80/20 targets* may include, but are not limited to, the following:

- *Heavy category users* – In the hair weave example, the hairstylist fits this description buying disproportionately more than anyone else. Winning with this *80/20 target* is the most intuitive way to go and works well when a dynamic like this is in play.

- *Key life stages* – The *Crest Whitestrips* example illustrates the life stage of getting married and the new considerations to go along with this transition. In my class, we also explored how getting married for women is a primary switching point for adding email addresses given that in the

United States, most brides change their names after marriage. Other life stage examples to consider are entering the workforce, having your first child, and becoming an empty nester.

- *Brand switchers* – When I worked on the *Folgers* brand, we had a sizable consumer base that was semi-loyal. More specifically, the consumer wanted to buy either *Folgers* or *Maxwell House.* The explanation was that she desired a trusted brand that would not embarrass her with guests, and either brand met that need. Although the purchase behavior was loyal, the consumer often reduced the brand to a description of *red can* and likewise *blue can* for *Maxwell House.* In this situation, the shopper decided in the retail aisle based on which brand had a lower price that day.

- *Point-of-Market-Entrants* – When consumers purchase in a category for the first time, they usually do their research. After they find a brand that satisfies their needs, those consumers may go years, or even decades, without considering another brand. At Procter & Gamble, an example of this dynamic played out in the deodorant category. Our deodorant brands would buy significant media weight to attract 15-year-old boys or girls, depending on the brand. After making their initial decisions, these consumers did not invest much time re-evaluating unless they had a bad experience. Note, this point-of-market-entry example happens to coincide with a new life stage, but this is not always the case. Whenever a consumer buys in a category for the first time, he or she is a point-of-market-entrant. Success comes from understanding what triggers the first purchase.

The above descriptions are common ways to identify *80/20 targets*. If you notice, the hair weave, *Whitestrips*, and dog food examples go beyond demographics and mindset to a specific behavior: installing hair extensions, preparing for a wedding, and celebrating the dog's birthday. We don't always get to this level, but this should be our goal.

Beyond the common ways to identify *80/20 targets*, the ideal *80/20 target* is the one uniquely meant for your brand. How do we determine this? It is easier than you might expect.

TWO CONSUMER IS BOSS

The 80/20 of Consumer Understanding

There is only one boss. The customer. And he can fire everybody in the company from the chairman on down, simply by spending his money somewhere else.

- Sam Walton

Consumer is Boss. This saying, plastered throughout the P&G headquarters during my time there, influenced the creation of the *80/20 target* designation and drove a more precise level of understanding. As we walked through the *80/20 target* examples, many people typically understood them in retrospect, but getting to these *80/20 targets* was not necessarily intuitive. In this chapter, we will use consumer data to identify our specific *80/20 target.*

OUR CONSUMER IS OUR BOSS

To know what the boss wants, we need to ask explicitly and listen intently. There are many tried and true ways to collect consumer data, including consumer focus groups, one-on-one interviews, shopper shelf studies, ethnographies, and the list goes on.

In this book, we will focus on surveys. These have worked dependably for clients over the years and for students every semester. Surveys are straightforward to create, using such tools as *Survey Monkey*, and may effortlessly be delivered to respondents using social media audiences, group distribution lists, or email contacts.

> *Note: The remainder of this chapter will walk through developing a survey structured for subsequent analysis. If you are not ready to create a survey for your brand, it is best to proceed to the next chapter and return when you are ready to build your survey.*

SURVEY STRATEGY

When given an opportunity to manage a brand, most people quickly create theories on how to improve the brand based on personal experiences or biases. A consumer survey allows you to test these theories and explore relevant areas where more information is helpful.

To help prepare for the survey, the students in my classes interview a representative of the brand. This experience is similar to the onboarding a brand manager has on a new brand. It is an opportunity to ask strategic questions for a more robust survey.

Common questions to consider:
- What is the biggest obstacle to growth for this brand?
- Who are the primary brand competitors?
- What sets this brand apart from the competition?
- What drives brand selection in this category?
- Who is the target and why?

The answers to these questions should be confirmed or denied with your consumer survey results.

DEMOGRAPHICS

Demographics are most commonly used to target consumers. This form of targeting is not the most sophisticated, but it is helpful for consumer visualization. On *Folgers*, for example, there are newly minted MBAs running a brand targeted to middle-aged consumers living in Middle America. We created a cardboard cutout of our target and named her Carol. Anytime we considered a new initiative or direction, the cutout of Carol grounded us in whether the idea was something 20-something MBAs wanted or something our consumer wanted.

From a survey structure perspective, some colleagues advocate placing demographic questions at the end of the survey. That works just as well. I keep the answering of these questions optional, although most respondents do not mind sharing.

Key demographic questions:

Age: *A typical format is below.*

    O Under 18

    O 18-24

    O 25-34

    O 35-44

    O 45-54

    O 55 or older

AARON HACKETT

Gender:

O Female

O Male

O Other (please specify)_____

Ethnicity: *In this question, allow respondents to select multiple races. Given the diverse culture of society, it gives a more nuanced picture.*

Ethnicity (check all that apply)

☐ Latino or Hispanic American

☐ White or Euro-American

☐ Black, Afro-Caribbean, or African American

☐ East Asian or Asian American

☐ South Asian or Indian American

☐ Middle Eastern or Arab American

☐ Native American or Alaskan Native

☐ Other

Education:
What is the highest degree or level of school you have completed?

O Less than a high school diploma or equivalent

O High school degree or equivalent

O Some college, no degree

O Associate degree

O Bachelor's degree

O Master's degree

O Doctorate

Marital status:

- O Single (never married)
- O Married, or in a domestic partnership
- O Widowed
- O Divorced
- O Separated

You may ask other demographic questions, but whether to include additional questions is a judgment call that balances the value of the data received and the length of the survey.

In this context, I define value based on how actionable the demographic information will be when you begin to target your consumer. For example, I rarely ask for household income. This demographic question tends to be tricky. Many respondents in the United States are more hesitant to share this information than the other demographic information listed. Although this question should be optional, this hesitation may be enough for a respondent to stop filling out the survey or to be less patient with subsequent questions that are more valuable to the brand. Another reason I rarely ask for household income is that I seldom see the value of this information when it comes to executing a marketing plan. Much of the value we would have received from the household income question, we also derive from other questions such as education level, age, and category behavior questions.

Managing survey length can improve the survey completion rate. Therefore, understanding the role of each question is vital. Consider how the answer to each question might affect your understanding of your consumer or influence your ultimate marketing activation. For example, if the demographic section is long, it may signal to respondents that they have a long survey ahead of them and may trigger early survey abandonment.

CATEGORY BEHAVIOR

Note that neither your brand nor its competitive brands have been mentioned to this point in the survey and should not be mentioned until we reach the Brand Specific Questions. We want to minimize bias. Correspondingly, the survey should not allude to your brand in the title nor the description.

The *Category Behavior* section serves to help a brand understand general inclinations toward a category. The questions should seek to gain attitudinal and behavior information from category participants. This section strives to elicit responses that identify a specific behavior that would set your *80/20 target* apart from general consumers. For example, in the Summer of 2018, a group of MBA students did their brand consulting project on *Warby Parker*. Below are the category behavior questions used:

For which of the following reasons do you use eyewear? Select all that apply.

☐ Corrective vision

☐ Sun protection

☐ Fashion (non-vision corrective)

☐ Wear Contacts

☐ Need vision correction, but go without

☐ Do not need vision correction

How often do you use eyewear for any reason?

O Daily

O 4-6 times a week

O 2-3 times a week

O Once a week

O Less than once a week

How often do you purchase eyewear?

O Multiple times a year

O Once a year

O Less than once a year

Where do you purchase eyewear? Select all that apply.

- ☐ Big box retail store
- ☐ Online
- ☐ Outlet mall
- ☐ Eye care provider
- ☐ Street vendors
- ☐ Mall kiosks

THE CORE QUESTION

The core question answers why a consumer buys a product in a category. It is critical to measure the level of importance for each decision attribute, rather than merely requesting a ranking, to create a robust core question. The ranking capability is a fun feature in most survey platforms, but the results from this feature tend to mislead brand managers. In many purchase decisions, consumers do not look at all the variables. That is not how shoppers think. We typically consider one or two factors that are most important to us and ignore the rest. Therefore, a consumer is more likely to share that one or two attributes are *Very Important* and the rest are *Not Important*. Yes, some consumers have thoughtfully considered many attributes of a purchase decision and can deliberately order these attributes with sound reasoning, but this is the exception rather than the rule. The preferences of this thoughtful consumer, along with the preferences of the more common consumer, may be precisely captured in a grid format.

Continuing with the *Warby Parker* example here is how this brand might structure the core question:

- When choosing eyewear, what factors are most important to you?

	Most Important	Very Important	Important	Slightly Important	Not Important
Style	O	O	O	O	O
Price	O	O	O	O	O
Brand	O	O	O	O	O
Customer Service	O	O	O	O	O
Convenience	O	O	O	O	O
Social Responsibility	O	O	O	O	O
Fit/comfort	O	O	O	O	O

It is best to structure the question attributes randomly to prevent attribute order from influencing answers.

COMPETITIVE QUESTIONS

The core question sets the structure for the competitive questions. This section is not a brainstorm session. It is merely an opportunity to compare identified competitors along the attributes selected in the *Core Question*. After learning what is most important in the consumer buying decision, the next step is to understand how your brand ranks in those attributes versus potential substitutes. For *Warby Parker*, the competitive questions may look like the ones below.

- ## How do you rate the following brands when it comes to style?

	Most Stylish	Very Stylish	Pretty Stylish	Not Very Stylish	Not Sure
Ray-Ban	o	o	o	o	o
Oakley	o	o	o	o	o
Warby Parker	o	o	o	o	o
Calvin Klein	o	o	o	o	o
Ralph Lauren	o	o	o	o	o
Dolce & Gabana	o	o	o	o	o
Brooks Brothers	o	o	o	o	o

The next question could be similar to this.

- ## How do rate the following brands when it comes to price?

	Most Expensive	Expensive	Moderately Priced	Inexpensive	Not Sure
Ralph Lauren	o	o	o	o	o
Warby Parker	o	o	o	o	o
Brooks Brothers	o	o	o	o	o
Oakley	o	o	o	o	o
Dolce & Gabana	o	o	o	o	o
Calvin Klein	o	o	o	o	o
Ray-Ban	o	o	o	o	o

- ## How would you rate the following eye-wear brands on their fit/comfort?

	Best Fit	Good Fit	OK Fit	Poor Fit	Not Sure
Calvin Klein	o	o	o	o	o
Dolce & Gabana	o	o	o	o	o
Ralph Lauren	o	o	o	o	o
Ray-Ban	o	o	o	o	o
Brooks Brothers	o	o	o	o	o
Warby Parker	o	o	o	o	o
Oakley	o	o	o	o	o

As with attributes in the core question, it is best to structure these questions in the survey to order competitors randomly. Similar questions for the remaining attributes would follow.

BRAND SPECIFIC QUESTIONS

This section is often not necessary unless the brand has a specific query, such as thoughts on a new logo. Many questions believed to be brand specific, turn out to be better served as additional competitive questions. For example, one may be curious about how recently a consumer may have purchased their brand. It would be more product- ive to ask a question such as, *How recently have you purchased any of the following brands?* and in- clude the competitive brands. When brand man- agers collect their brand-specific information on a metric like purchase recency, the natural desire is to compare the response for the brand with the responses of its primary competitors. This style of questioning also conceals your brand from re- spondents, helping to minimize bias.

In the scenario which warrants specific brand questions, placing those questions at the end of the survey lessens the likelihood of respondent bias.

The vast majority of responses come in the first week. I have rarely seen input after the first week significantly alter survey results. This survey structure allows us to deliberately break down the most salient aspects of your brand *positioning*. Brand *positioning* is the key to building a meaningful brand.

THREE LESS IS MORE

The 80/20 of Positioning

Simple can be harder than complex: You have to work hard to get your thinking clean to make it simple. But it's worth it in the end because once you get there, you can move mountains.

- *Steve Jobs*

The origin of the phrase *less is more* is widely attributed to Robert Browning who used it in his poem *Andrea del Sarto* in 1855. *Less is more* describes the beauty of clean, uncluttered design. The concept of *less is more* goes beyond design into how we engage as shoppers.

Psychologists Sheena Iyengar and Mark Lepper published a study on jam that reinforced this view in 2002. The structure was straightforward. Shoppers sampled jam flavors in the same store on different days. After sampling, shoppers on both days received a one-dollar-off coupon for jam. The only difference was that on the first day shoppers sampled twenty-four flavors of jam, but on the second day, shoppers only sampled six flavors. What did Iyengar and Lepper find? The display with twenty-four jam flavors attracted more shopper interest, but the shoppers who sampled from the six jam flavors were ten times more likely to purchase. The lesson is to prevent the shopper from working too hard. This mantra also played out in subtle ways at Procter & Gamble.

THE P&G ONE-PAGER

The structure and focus at Procter & Gamble pushed our business decisions in powerful ways. If an assistant brand manager wanted to make a brand recommendation, he or she needed to outline the rationale on a single page document. With so many brands, decision-makers needed recommendations simplified to their essential elements. Most of us took a two-day memo writing course called *Leadership on Paper* to assist in acquiring the skill of single-page document persuasion. According to the President and Founder of *Leadership on Paper*, Jean Paul Plumez, *Good ideas are invariably strengthened on paper and weak ideas are exposed for what they are*. In that spirit, we organized our one-pagers in the following manner:

- *Recommendation* – What you propose in a

single sentence.

- *Background* – Only the areas which are most relevant to your recommendation and have general agreement.
- *Description* – Key details of the proposal; who, what, how, when, where.
- *Basis for Recommendation* – The three key benefits in priority order.
- *Next Steps* – What actions will be taken by whom and when upon approval.

To confine your brand recommendation to a single page, when it might require millions of dollars in resources, you must clarify your thinking. In such little space, you do not list every reason that supports your argument, only the most compelling. You find ways to organize your thoughts into buckets which are easy for the reader to digest. Through the clarification process, you refine your thinking and simultaneously improve your grasp of the recommendation. The rumor was that an assistant brand manager in the laundry category wrote a one-pager that initiated the transition from P&G's suit and tie culture to its business casual work environment. The reasoning was that if P&G employees wore business casual attire, employees would benefit by saving on their dry cleaning bills but P&G would benefit from the increased usage of *Tide* by tens of thousands of employees translating into a sizable on-going revenue increase.

Simplicity is an important concept to keep in mind when advertising to your *80/20 target* and definitely before beginning data analysis. We will create simplicity through structure. There will be interesting tidbits in your survey you may follow, but first, it is essential to organize the data in an easy to consume format. Before starting this journey, it is vital to understand our destination. Our survey was explicitly structured to provide us the data for the most fundamental brand assessment concept. This concept is brand *positioning*.

BRAND POSITIONING

Positioning should be your primary brand strategy tool. When I engage with a new brand, *positioning* is where my mind naturally goes. Many brands miss this, but it is reasonably intuitive. We will walk through the logic of *positioning* using *Tom's of Maine* toothpaste for illustrative purposes. For those not familiar with *Tom's of Maine*, it is a natural brand that boasts on its website, *Finding Natural Solutions: At Tom's of Maine, we believe you shouldn't have to choose between effectiveness and a naturally healthy life. For over 45 years, we've searched the world for ingredients and combined them in fresh new ways to create natural products that work.*

The way we walk through *positioning* is how a brand manager would typically think through a brand's *positioning*, but we will later reorder this exploration in a way that is easier to remember.

- **What about my brand makes it unique?** – How does your brand improve the targets experience above his or her current solution? The answer to this question serves are your **point of difference (POD)**. It is common for a brand to claim multiple *PODs* but lean towards focusing on the most meaningful *POD*. For *Tom's of Maine* toothpaste, what makes this brand unique is the natural ingredients. Many of their SKUs are fluoride-free, which happens to be the exact opposite of what many people look for in a toothpaste.

- **Who would find this POD most appealing?** – Given that we have grown up with an understanding that fluoride is essential for healthy teeth, this consumer tends to fall in the minority. This is not a bad thing. As we mentioned in chapter one, it is better for 20% of the population to love you and 80% to hate you than for everyone to like you. The **80/20 target** who would love this brand would be the minority that is open to the idea that fluoride is possibly not essential for healthy teeth and maybe even of the mindset that it is a toxin that is hazardous to your health. However, what is the behavior of someone who is more conscious than most of the possible toxins they might encounter? As I have run this case study, certain behaviors such as using natural shampoo or using natural deodorants have had a high correlation with people who have tried this brand. The most common behavior that tips off a consumer who might be in your *80/20 target* is an overwhelming bias to buy organic foods.

· **If your 80/20 target chooses a different brand, which brands would they most likely be?** These brands will serve as your **competitive set**. For the example of *Tom's of Maine* toothpaste, student tendency is to assume the *80/20 target* would choose between *Tom's of Maine* and another natural toothpaste brand such as *Jason*. However, over and over again, we see that the majority of consumers who try *Tom's of Maine* were not choosing between natural toothpaste brands, but instead versus their current brand, most commonly *Crest* or *Colgate*. Given that 80% of the toothpaste market uses these major brands, this category has not changed enough for *Tom's of Maine* to be primarily concerned about other natural brands.

· **What is the primary attribute your 80/20 target uses to compare brands in**

your competitive set? This attribute is your **point of parity (POP).** It is common to have multiple *POPs* but pay particular attention to which *POP* matters most. Consider which *POP* might be used in messaging. A *POP* may also be considered a price of entry in many situations. Given that *Tom's of Maine* would most likely be compared with *Crest* or *Colgate*, the *POP* historically would have been cavity protection, but more recently seems to have evolved to whitening.

This example explores vital questions that a brand manager would want to answer as he or she develops a brand strategy. For ease of memory, the brand *positioning* may be summarized by the following four bullet points:

- *80/20 Target*
- *Competitive Set*
- *Point of Parity (POP)*
- *Point of Difference (POD)*

In case you are interested in how well this narrowly targeted toothpaste brand is doing, *Colgate* identified this trend in natural toothpaste over a decade ago and bought controlling interest of the *Tom's of Maine* brand for $100 million in 2006.

Competitive Perspective:

Competition is commonly assessed along the dimension of category. It is important to note that while category works in the vast majority of situations, it is not the most precise way to define the *competitive set*. *Benefit* and *80/20 target* are more enlightening than the category.

Red Bull – When exploring *competitors* of *Red Bull*, typical examples are *Monster*, *Rockstar*, and *NOS*, which happen to all be in the energy drink segment. However, another common *competitor* is *Starbucks* coffee. Although coffee is in a different segment, consumers also use these beverages to help them push through a lull. Consumers are more interested in the benefit than the segment or category.

Pampers – What about *Pampers* and *Luvs* diapers? While these brands are in the same category and switching may exist between the two brands, it is minimal. My Procter & Gamble internship was with *Luvs* diapers. What I saw from consumer research and in the data was that *Luvs* diapers consumers rarely also bought *Pampers*. The *80/20 targets* for these brands ironically were in different life stages. The *Pampers 80/20 target* is the first time Mom who has just entered this magical stage of becoming a mother. Her life and perspective are abruptly altered. She has a new responsibility that she cherishes, yet little experience in this area. Therefore, she looks to minimize risks and do whatever might be necessary for her new little treasure. The premium *Pampers* brand has all of the bells and whistles including the best lotions for sensitive skin and a clothlike back-sheet to make diapers feel more luxurious. The *Luvs 80/20 target*, on the other hand, is a mother with multiple children. She respects the responsibility of motherhood every bit as much but has the experience and confidence to discriminate between what is necessary for her little one and where she should invest the family budget. She foregoes bells and whistles for the category *POP* of leakage protection. When I was on *Luvs*, the tagline was *Live and Learn and then get Luvs* as a head nod to prudently buying what you need.

Point of Difference Perspective:

A brand's *POD* is where it connects to the *80/20 target*. There is a school of thought that winning entails creating a new category, as is described in the book, *Zero to One* by Peter Thiel and Blake Masters. I suggest that the primary difference in this school of thought and what I am sharing is semantics. If your *POD* is meaningful and differentiated enough, that *POD* may be perceived as a new category. Where I diverge is that even if you create a category of one, this does not mean you do not have any *competition*. If your brand, the category of one, does not exist, the consumer will often make another selection. The brands selected most often are your *competition*.

PERCEPTUAL MAPPING

Perceptual mapping is one of the many charting techniques used to illustrate a competitive landscape. A nice feature of this technique is that it may be used as a visualization tool for brand *positioning*. This visualization allows a brand to use a perceptual map as a single image for displaying its strategy. Here is how we convert brand *positioning* into a perceptual map.

- *80/20 Target* – The *80/20 target* is not explicitly illustrated in the map, but each map should be grounded in a single *80/20 target*. Therefore, we want to exclude data in this map from anyone not identified as your *80/20 target*. Many maps include the feedback of all consumers, but focused targeting allows for a more precise map. Remember, our most important efforts are to build advocacy with our *80/20 target* even if it hurts us with the general population. Some brands compensate for the implicit nature of the *80/20 target* by placing her or his picture in a corner of the perceptual map.
- *Competitive Set* – The *competition* should be limited to the *competitors* that matter most. This level of importance is based on the likelihood of the *80/20 target* to

purchase these *competitors* if the option of your brand is not available. In other words, which other brands would best meet the needs of your *80/20 target*.

- *Point of Parity (POP)* – This is one axis of the perceptual map. Not what makes your brand unique, but what the *80/20 target* seeks during the purchase decision.
- *Point of Difference (POD)* – This is the other perceptual map axis. Your brand will perform well in this dimension. This helps us understand how well you are delivering versus the *competitive set* and which *competitors* threaten your level of uniqueness. Success here is critical as this is the reason for *80/20 target* appeal.

These are the fundamental components of the perceptual map, your *strategy in an image*. We will use this image to assess and guide your *brand equity*.

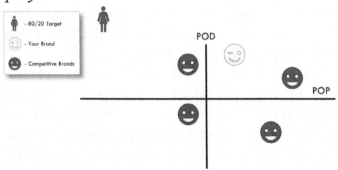

The perceptual map captures the components of positioning using the 80/20 target as the reference

Brand equity may be the most commonly used term in brand management. Think of it as the value beyond that of a generic category product derived from consumer perceptions of the brand. This incremental value holds even when the product is from the same manufacturer and is of similar quality.

In 2005, Procter & Gamble was dealt a body blow. At the time, *Costco* carried the two leading premium diaper brands, *Pampers* and *Huggies*. *Costco* decided to enter as a private label brand in this profitable category, so approached both manufacturers about a sourcing agreement for the *Kirkland Signature* diaper initiative. Procter & Gamble declined the offer with minimal consideration, but Kimberly Clark accepted. In what seemed like overnight, one of P&G's multi-billion-dollar brands lost complete distribution at the largest warehouse retailer in the United States.

But this story is not about *Pampers*, it is about *Huggies*, and more specifically, the *Huggies brand equity*. The *Kirkland Signature* diaper is manufactured by Kimberly Clark, yet *Huggies* clears around a 30% price premium. *Costco* shoppers compare both diaper brands, and many decide to pay 30% more when comparing diapers that have the same diaper count per box for a given size, making the math simpler. As I have inquired about this launch with multiple past and current Kimberly Clark employees, including co-workers and students, they have consistently told me that the *Kirkland Signature* brand was even from a higher quality line than the *Huggies* line sold right next to it at *Costco*. I cannot validate if this is still the case but if we believe this assertion, shoppers are paying more money for a lower-quality option. This is the magic of *brand equity*.

Price is only one way to measure *brand equity.* We use the *point of difference* and the *point of parity* as another way to measure it. Where your brand lies in your perceptual map sheds light on your *brand equity*. Luckily, *brand equity* is not static. We can build it in a way that is most meaningful to the *80/20 target* with *messaging* and product initiatives. The survey results provide what you need to create your *strategy in an image*. Let's roll up our sleeves and interpret the data.

FOUR MARKETERS LIE, BUT NUMBERS DON'T

The 80/20 of Analysis

Without data, you're just another person with an opinion.

- *W. Edwards Deming*

As a Procter & Gamble assistant brand manager, I learned that my recommendations were not compelling unless data backed them. Everyone on a brand has a gut instinct. Without data, the gut instinct of the most senior marketer, the person with the most stripes, wins. Data is how a young brand person gains influence.

Marketing guru Seth Godin wrote a book called *All Marketers are Liars*, sometimes referred to as *All Marketers are Storytellers*. The takeaway is that consumers engage with brands through stories. Consumers do not naturally make decisions through the analytical breakdown of the facts but through the emotional connection of a story. Stories are how we learn and relate. The desire for stories in our culture is pervasive, from television to movies to novels. The most influential brand stories are grounded in consumer insights and data. Numbers don't lie, and a savvy brand builder knows how to weave the data into a compelling story. We will pinpoint the shortcuts to analyzing your survey data and how this data lays the foundation for your brand story.

Note: The remainder of this chapter will walk through getting the most meaningful strategic direction out of the survey responses. If you have not yet fielded a survey, it is best to proceed to the next chapter and return when you are ready to analyze survey results.

SURVEY ANALYSIS

What about my brand makes it unique? The consumer answers this question in the *Competitive Questions* portion of the survey. Recall that you asked how the respondent rated the brands versus each aspect of the core question. As you review the questions in this section, which aspect sets your brand apart from the *competition*? Unfortunately, sometimes the answer is none. You may not rate the best in any of these areas. When your brand is not judged to be the best in any aspect, you may find the aspect where your brand performs relatively well. You may also find the area where you believe your brand does not rate well because of an error in perception. In this situation, your marketing should help improve this suboptimal perception. Sometimes the brand is best in multiple areas. When your brand is the best in more than one aspect, decide which one is more strategically important to your long-term success.

In our *Warby Parker* example, the brand benefitted from the best rating in multiple aspects. Warby Parker scored highest in *style*, *convenience*, *customer service*, and *social responsibility*. In contrast, the brand scored second in *fit/comfort* and a distant third in *price*. Strategically, it made sense to go with *style* as *Warby Parker's POD* for a couple of reasons.

Style was the competitive question with the greatest absolute and relative advantage versus alternatives when respondents rated a brand to be *Extremely Good*.

- *Style* – Absolute (24%) and relative (+12 percentage points versus next best brand)
- *Convenience* - Absolute (14%) and relative (+4 percentage points versus next best brand)
- *Customer service* - Absolute (13%) and relative (+4 percentage points versus next best brand)
- *Social responsibility* - Absolute (3%) and relative (+1 percentage point versus next best brand)

Another method is using the importance of the attribute in the *Core Question*. *Style* was the second most important attribute to respondents overall falling behind only *fit/comfort*, which was one of the few attributes where *Warby Parker* did not score highest.

Who would find this POD most appealing? The rule of thumb is that the *80/20 target* should represent somewhere between 10% to 30% of the respondents. There is more than one way to use survey data to find an *80/20 target*, but the most straightforward way is to isolate the respondents who cared the most for your *POD*. We can find this information in the *Core Question*.

In the *Warby Parker* example, the *POD* is *style*. There were 28% of respondents that said *style* was *Most Important*. There are situations when one might choose the top two options, *Most Important* and *Very Important*, but 28% fits nicely in our 10% to 30% window. Adding the top two options in this example would be 66% representing the majority rather than the most passionate segment.

At this point in the analysis, we make a critical cut of the data. My students use *Qualtrics* because of the ease of filtering, but this may be done by downloading to a spreadsheet, if necessary. Cut the data by filtering the data on only your *80/20 target*. For *Warby Parker*, we filter for the *80/20 target* by going to the *Core Question* and filtering only for respondents that answered that *Style* was *Most Important* when choosing glasses. We care specifically about their responses to the survey questions and need to be able to review them apart from, and in comparison to, the answers of the total respondents.

Now compare the *Demographics* section for the *80/20 target* versus the *Demographics* section for total respondents. Pay attention to the most significant changes in gender, age, and other demographic descriptions. When comparing data, relative comparisons are most important. For example, if 10% of the total survey respondents are female, but 40% of the *80/20 target* respondents are female, the *80/20 target* is most likely female. Even though less than half of the *80/20 target* from your data is female, this subsegment is four times more likely to be female than the total population of respondents.

This method of comparison serves as a normalizing factor. Although targeting based on behavior is ideal, demographic skews should be leveraged to the extent feasible.

From the demographic data, craft a visual identity for your target, similar to the example shared from the *Folgers* brand about Carol. The easiest way is to search the internet and copy images of people that you believe represent the *80/20 target* that your data describes. This visual serves as a guidepost when making strategic brand decisions and is helpful when casting people for advertising purposes.

The *Warby Parker 80/20 target* tended to be in the 25 to 34 age range (68% in the *80/20 target* data versus 54% in the overall data) and single (55% in the *80/20 target* data versus 45% in the overall data). The data was too close for gender and education to make a designation.

Next, compare the *Category Behavior* section for the *80/20 target* versus the *Category Behavior* section for total respondents. Here is where we sometimes find the critical behavior differences that set the *80/20 target* apart.

The *Warby Parker 80/20 target* was most likely to use eyewear for sun protection, but the overall group was most likely to use eyewear for vision correction. Correspondingly, the *80/20 target* was less likely to purchase their eyewear from an eye care provider (29% versus 41%). This low percentage hints at an opportunity for broader distribution with optometrists.

If your 80/20 target chooses a different brand, which brands would they most likely be? To answer this question, we would typically look at the 80/20 data only. Go to the *Competitive Question* that specifically rates your *POD*. In this question, the *competitors* that also rate well are most commonly your *key competitors*. However, this is not always the case. In our *Tom's of Maine* example, the key *competitors* are *Crest* and *Colgate*, *competitors* that rate poorly in *Tom's of Maine's POD*, but lead the *competitive set* in the *POP*. There are shortcuts to help make this decision, but the dynamics of each category dictate how to approach this question.

What is the primary attribute your 80/20 target uses to compare brands in your competitive set? If your brand truly has an innovative *POD*, the *POP* would be the common preference before the introduction of your brand to the *80/20 target*. Generally, it is the *Core Question* answer that has the most significant level of importance in the purchase decision.

From our *Warby Parker* example, we take the *80/20 target*-only data and find the *Core Question*. The *most important* aspect of this data for eyewear purchase decision was *style* (100% by definition of our *POD*), followed by *fit/comfort* (56%). Although significantly behind *style*, *fit/comfort* was over 30 percentage points ahead of the third next aspect of *convenience* (24%). For perspective, the *POP* of *fit/comfort* happened to be the *most important* purchase decision factor when looking at the data from all respondents.

PERCEPTUAL MAP CREATION

After using the data to answer key *80/20 target* questions, we can go one layer deeper to create a perceptual map. Remember, this perceptual map will be *80/20 target* specific, rather than depict the perceptions of all respondents. Putting an image of your *80/20 target* in the top left corner of your paper is helpful. There is a natural desire to include the broader data to create a more general perceptual map, but we are intensely interested in the thoughts of our *80/20 target*. Overall perceptions are interesting, but they are not nearly as important as those of the *80/20 target*.

The two axes will be that of your *POD* and your *POP*. Go to the *Competitive Questions* section of your *80/20 target* data and get the data from the questions for only the attributes that you use as *POD* and *POP*.

In our *Warby Parker POD* example, this was the *POD* question: *How do you rate the following brands when it comes to style?*

	Most Stylish	Very Stylish	Pretty Stylish	Not Very Stylish	Not Sure
Ray-Ban	o	o	o	o	o
Oakley	o	o	o	o	o
Warby Parker	o	o	o	o	o
Calvin Klein	o	o	o	o	o
Ralph Lauren	o	o	o	o	o
Dolce & Gabana	o	o	o	o	o
Brooks Brothers	o	o	o	o	o

For each option assign a numeric value as below:
- *Most stylish = 2*
- *Very stylish = 1*
- *Pretty stylish = -1*
- *Not very stylish =-2*

Ignore the *not sure* responses for this exercise. Multiply the number of responses for each answer by the assigned value and then divide the sum of these values by the total number of responses (not including *not sure* responses) to get an average for each brand.

Do the same thing with your *POP* question:

How would you rate the following eyewear brands on their fit/comfort?

	Best Fit	Good Fit	OK Fit	Poor Fit	Not Sure
Calvin Klein	o	o	o	o	o
Dolce & Gabana	o	o	o	o	o
Ralph Lauren	o	o	o	o	o
Ray-Ban	o	o	o	o	o
Brooks Brothers	o	o	o	o	o
Warby Parker	o	o	o	o	o
Oakley	o	o	o	o	o

For each option assign a numeric value as below:
- *Best fit = 2*
- *Good fit = 1*
- *OK fit = -1*
- *Poor fit = -2*

Again, ignore the *not sure* responses for this exercise. Multiply the number of responses for each answer by the assigned value and then divide the sum of these values by the total number of responses (not including *not sure* responses) to get an average for each brand.

At this point, you have the numeric values for each brand on your *POD* and *POP* axes and may plot the brands in an X, Y manner.

This graph simplifies competitive complexity into a single image. Moving your brand on this map going forward is predominantly a function of your messaging but may also be influenced by such factors as initiative launches. This movement is, in effect, managing your *brand equity*.

FIVE OPPORTUNITY FROM CHAOS

The 80/20 of Messaging

In the midst of chaos, there is also opportunity.

\-   *Sun Tzu*

As I was ending my first assistant brand manager assignment, my brand manager, Gary DeJesus, gave me *The Art of War* by Sun Tzu. This book was the same gift extended to him after his first assistant brand manager role. Gary chose to continue this gesture because of the wisdom he gleaned from the book and its relevance to the hectic life of a Procter & Gamble assistant brand manager.

Sun Tzu was a Chinese general of the period around 500 BC. He was a widely revered military strategist who professed that it was better to win a battle without fighting than to win in combat. Even in victory, the winner bears the loss of military lives, the depletion of ammunition, and, depending on battle location, destruction of property. One of Sun Tzu's most enduring quotes is *In the midst of chaos, there is also opportunity*. This quote applies to many situations in life, and specifically in brand management. Chaos surrounds brands in the form of competitive threats, shifting trends, evolving consumer behaviors, changing cost structures, and the list goes on. The ability to find an opportunity and exploit it in the face of this chaos is what sets the great brand managers apart. Uncovering *opportunity from chaos* is especially meaningful in brand messaging. Even slight miscalculations in messaging may mean the difference between success and failure.

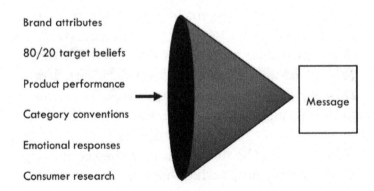

FEBREZE LAUNCH

Most people are aware of the multi-billion-dollar *Febreze* brand. However, most people do not know how close this brand came to never launching. In a Procter & Gamble training session, I learned the details of this predicament.

Febreze was a highly anticipated brand that went to test markets in Boise, Idaho; Phoenix, Arizona; and Salt Lake City, Utah in preparation for a national launch. Unfortunately, test market results did not meet expectations. The concept played well with consumers in initial testing but did not translate to test market sales. As the brand team explored this issue, they found a seemingly minor nuance in the marketing message. In test markets, the message was *Febreze traps odors*, true to the Research and Development technical description of the process. After tweaking the message to *Febreze cleans away odor*, sales rebounded. The consumer perception of trapping odors was not nearly as motivating as cleaning away odors. The idea of trapping suggested that the odor was still there. Although the technology did not change, *Febreze* changed the description of the technology. This example emphasizes how precise messaging must be in some instances.

Branding is about telling a story. Your marketing message is the central way of sharing this story.

We underestimate the difficulty in creating this message. Students and clients alike often value cleverness over precision. The challenge in creating a compelling message is grounded in translating *science* into *art*.

CHAOS AND OPPORTUNITY

Companies like Procter & Gamble invest significant time and money into understanding the consumer and into gathering data. In many cases, brands have too much of a good thing. Brand builders must decide which negative data points are acceptable and do not merit focus, while mining data for the insights that most motivate the *80/20 target*. After selecting the insight to pursue, brand builders must be careful to communicate this benefit effectively. Avoid the *Febreze* pitfall.

Reputable creative agencies make their money transforming key consumer insights into award-winning messaging. Messaging is where we transition from *science* to *art* in brand management. Most brands cannot afford top-tier creative agencies, so must be able to create compelling messaging independently. Even brand builders from companies such as Procter & Gamble who have easy access to creative agencies benefit from the ability to develop meaningful messaging. Brand builders must provide creative agencies with strategic direction and insightful feedback on the work produced. In my career, I have found that envisioning a message that met the deliverables of a creative brief enabled more robust dialogue around subsequent creative work.

The skill of messaging is one that builds over time with practice. A consistent structure helps to develop competency.

MARKETING OBJECTIVE

The *marketing objective* merely is what the brand would like to accomplish with its *80/20 target* when creating a marketing plan. When it comes to *marketing objectives*, I have heard dozens proposed by clients and students. In my experience, three *marketing objectives* cover brand needs 80% of the time. These *marketing objectives* are *awareness*, *trial*, and *repeat*. Of course, you may come up with more exciting or clever sounding *marketing objectives* than these three, but when it comes down to it, using these three in the overwhelming majority of marketing plans will help you deliver the results your brand seeks. *Awareness*, *trial*, and *repeat* work as a funnel with *awareness* preceding *trial* and *trial* followed by *repeat*.

- *Awareness* – Brand *awareness* tends to be the most common *marketing objective* because most brands are smaller and less known. *Awareness* tends to be a function of marketing media weight. Media spend is the default lever for controlling *awareness* levels. *Awareness* may be bucketed in a few ways.
    - *Unaided recall* – Naming a brand after being asked to list brands in a given category or that deliver a specific benefit.
    - *Aided recall* – If a brand is not listed during the first question, a follow-up question such as have you heard of this brand may be asked. At this point, *awareness* is categorized as aided.
    - *Depth of awareness* – Depth measures how quickly a respondent mentions a brand when given a

category.

- ○ *Breadth of awareness* – This is a measure of how many categories respondents recognize for a brand.

- *Trial* – *Trial* is the act of getting people to experience your brand. The first time a consumer purchases the brand is the purest form of *trial*. A few points of clarification around *trial*.

  - ○ Sampling is a common form of *trial*, especially in the food and beverage categories.
  - ○ In the automobile category, a test drive may be considered *trial*.
  - ○ When a brand strives to build *awareness* of features, the *marketing objective* is likely *trial*. Typically, in this situation the *80/20 target* is already *aware* of the brand, so the *objective* would no longer be *awareness*. Building feature *awareness* is a tactic for motivating a consumer to *try* the brand.
  - ○ In-Store purchase leverages an element of *trial* Procter & Gamble calls *First Moment of Truth (FMOT)*. We explain *FMOT* in chapter seven.

- *Repeat* – This *objective* focuses on getting the *80/20 target* to continue buying the brand. *Repeat* is where Product Development earns its money in the consumer packaged goods world. Here are tactics for driving *repeat*.

- *Loyalty programs*, such as the type popularized by the airline industry. Such programs may include loyalty cards that provide a benefit after a certain level of purchase.
- *Experience continuity* is when a consumer *repeats* for a guaranteed experience. This experience may range from knowing your *Big Mac* will taste the same from any *McDonald's* in the country to more involved experiences such as ensuring your next *iPhone* will automatically replicate from the older model when you are ready for an upgrade.
- There is the *refill model*. Often cited examples include ink for your printer, blades for your razor, and toothbrush heads for your electric toothbrush.
- More traditional targeted promotions will contact the consumer around the anticipated time of re-purchase. Tools such as email marketing are valuable in this area.

ACCEPTED CONSUMER BELIEF

The key to effective messaging is gaining the insight to influence our *80/20 target*. If we want her to be aware of us, what should we say to motivate our *80/20 target* enough to add us to her *consideration set*? If we want her to *try* us, what is it that makes her believe she may have an experience that is better than her current experience? If we want her to continue purchasing us, how do we remind her of why she chose us and how we can continue providing value?

At Procter & Gamble, we grounded our messaging in the *accepted consumer belief*. Understanding what a consumer believes about a category guides brand direction. Understanding her unmet needs will unveil the *opportunity from within the chaos*. Looking back at our survey, we were able to identify our *80/20 target* and sort her responses from those of the broader group of responses. The places where the *80/20 target* significantly departed from the total group helped us to understand what was unique about her. In our *Warby Parker* example, the most important attribute for our *80/20 target* in our *Core Question* was *style*, while the most important attribute for the general population was *fit/comfort*. *Style* was unsurpassed in this category for our *80/20 target* and most likely essential in other areas of her life. Therefore, when creating a print ad, *style* would be a critical component that should not be limited to the eyeglasses but should play out in every aspect of the communication from clothing choices to background elements in the *Warby Parker* ad. The *accepted consumer belief* helps us better use the perceptual map to move from the *science* of our analysis to the *art* of the message.

FROM SCIENCE TO ART

The message is one of the most strategic aspects of brand building. You have significant information about your brand. If you had a ten-minute conversation with a consumer, you would probably be successful in getting her to *try* your brand. Of course, this is not feasible from a marketing perspective, and a consumer will only give you mere seconds. The message must be engaging to earn her attention. Therefore, delivering a concise message that goes to the heart of her *accepted consumer belief* is mandatory.

When assessing the effectiveness of student presentations, I put more emphasis on the message than any other portion of the project because the message is the point of connection between the brand and the consumer. Big brands condense their pitches down to 30-second television commercials. Smaller brands may be limited to a print ad that hopefully engages the consumer enough to get her to stop and pay attention. The print ad must also connect with the consumer through her *accepted consumer belief* to ultimately meet the *marketing objective* of *awareness*, *trial*, or *repeat*. The *80/20 target* must interpret the message quickly, so the different aspects must reinforce each other.

Express the advertising idea through the fundamental elements of your message: *headline, image*, and *reason to believe.*

- *Headline (Say it)* – Be precise, rather than cute. We commonly see clever *headlines* we love. Keep in mind that brands with heavier media weights can more effectively use these because consumers have a base understanding of what the brand has to offer. Most brands do not benefit from a high level of familiarity. You will have a wealth of information about your brand but avoid the temptation to detail all the brand has to offer. Communicate what is most important to your *80/20 target* based on your *marketing objective*. Attempting to communicate five benefits is a recipe for not effectively communication any. Always speak in consumer-friendly language. Do not slip in marketing or category lingo. The best *headlines* are heart-opening or mind-opening.
- *Image (Show it)* – A picture is worth a thousand words. The *image* is usually the most engaging part of your message and almost

always noticed first. Make it work hard, using it to reinforce your *headline*. You may consider using an *image* to communicate a benefit different than that of the *headline* to sell consumers on what else your brand has to offer, but this often causes confusion rather than broader communication.

People are frequently a part of the *image*. Given this, here are a few notes to keep in mind concerning demographic casting. As you would expect, beginning with the demographics of your *80/20 target* is appropriate. Adjustments from this base may be affected by a few things.

○ *Aspiration* – Adjust towards the demographic that the *80/20 target* finds aspirational. Older consumers aspire to be young again, especially when casting for beauty or anti-aging products. Tweens aspire to be teens or adults. Deodorant ads targeting teens employ this tactic. Skinny male teens tend to want to be more muscular young men.

○ *Black consumers* – When I worked as Procter & Gamble's Multicultural brand manager, I learned that Black consumers were likely to ignore ads that did not have Black talent. This tendency was because Black consumers sometimes had specific desires in areas like beauty care or entertainment. As a minority group of about 13% of the United States population, this consumer expected that an ad would not be specifically for them without Black talent.

- *White consumers* – Conversely, White consumers expected that all ads were for them. This expectation allowed ethnic casting to have a minimal negative effect with White consumers. This logic bolstered talent casting of minority groups in the early 2000s.
- *Generally appealing ethnicity* – Our work also uncovered that the most broadly accepted ethnicity was a talent mix of White and Asian. When a brand is not sure which ethnic direction to go, this representation is less risky.

In your *image, benefit visualization* is even more important than casting. Here are a few established approaches:

- *Before and After* – Demonstrate the current state versus the desired state. The early *Tide* advertising used this method of benefit visualization in the iconic advertising showing pants with grass stains next to pants cleaned with Tide. If pushed to choose between visualizing the problem or solution, lean towards the solution. An *image* of the problem may connect to consumer motivation, but the lack of resolution tends to be unpersuasive.

◦ *Torture Test* - Reassure a consumer that your brand will deliver a benefit by using a worst-case scenario. On the *Luvs* brand, we would subtly insert a father with a baby on his shoulders. The *Luvs* benefit was *no leaking*. If a father had any doubt about a diaper leaking, he would not put the baby on his shoulders. The downside is too great.

◦ *Emotional Connection* - Michelin is one of the most highly regarded brands in the automotive tire category. Many do not credit this success to an advertising campaign that glorified the tire tread quality. No, not because Michelin promised your car would hug the roads during sharp turns or wick water away in the rain. Instead, Michelin is applauded for the brand building marketing campaign with the *headline - Michelin. Because so much is riding on your tires.* The *image* was of a baby sitting inside a tire. No metrics were necessary. A heart-opening visual that removed any doubt that your tire choice was paramount.

◦ *Consumer Context* - Paint a picture in consumer minds of the situation where your brand will help most. In the spirit of 80/20, avoid selling them on broad usage occasions. The *Downy Wrinkle Releaser* example that follows illustrates this point.

• *Reason to Believe (Support it)* – This is the opportunity to back up your claim. Consumers are skeptical of marketing claims, so supplementing a message with a *reason to believe* may sway your target. Common *reasons to believe* include test data, expert confirmation, or a simple explanation. Brands may also offer a *call to action* such as a money-back guarantee.

The *headline, image,* and *reason to believe* should reinforce each other rather than attempt to communicate multiple benefits. Do not be afraid to focus sharply on how a consumer should use your product.

When I worked at a private equity firm, I led Procter & Gamble's *Downy Wrinkle Releaser* business through a licensing relationship. *Downy Wrinkle Releaser* addressed a consumer tension. Consumers wanted to look neat, yet hated to iron. The concept of spraying wrinkles away was effective for driving *trial,* but *repeat* remained an issue. Research led us to understand that consumers were buying the product, however not using it. By all accounts, they liked the benefit. They simply forgot about the product. To drive *repeat,* we created a message focused on usage context. The benefit of wrinkle elimination for clothes was too general. We narrowed our sights on using *Downy Wrinkle Releaser* as the perfect companion for business trips and created a three-ounce travel-friendly version. The routine of packing a suitcase became a reminder for *Downy Wrinkle Releaser*. The previous communication that *Downy Wrinkle Releaser* was perfect for all wrinkle situations, translated to its use in no wrinkle situations. Conversely, consumers who used *Downy Wrinkle Releaser* on trips found other situations for using the product.

Here is an example of a print ad that integrates the

headline, image, and *reason to believe* to address an *accepted consumer belief.*

- *Accepted Consumer Belief* – If my hair is healthy it should not break but be resilient and strong.
- *Headline* – *10X Stronger Hair* is concise and communicates a magnitude of the benefit which is quickly understood. The *10X* is *mind-opening,* altering our expectations of how strong hair can be.
- *Image* – A woman pulling on her hair is a literal demonstration of its strength along with the health assumed from the *accepted consumer belief.* The *image* is a logical visualization of the *headline.*
- *Reason to Believe* – Pro-Vitamin image, *Pantene's* proprietary ingredient for healthy hair.

DO NOT LOSE THE INSIGHT

Putting together a *headline, image,* and *reason to believe* seems straightforward. The message is meant to tell a story based on an *accepted consumer belief* that will motivate your *80/20 target*. Unfortunately, the transformation from *science* to *art* takes on a form that sometimes lacks evidence of the robust data that led to the insight. As confirmation that the *art* of the message retains much of the *science*, here are three checks for proper translation.

- *Consistency* - Are the *headline, image,* and *reason to believe* reinforcing each other or communicating different things? It is tempting to try to sell all of the brand benefits, but your best chance of success is selling a single benefit convincingly.
- *Precision* - Is the message specifically addressing the *accepted consumer belief*? This specificity goes to the heart of why the *80/20 target* should choose your brand. Given the research and learning about your consumer, this message should drive to the heart of her desire.
- *Engagement* - Would this message grab the *80/20 target's* attention? Is it *heart-opening* (makes you feel) or *mind-opening* (makes you think)? From a *YouTube* per-

spective, make your *80/20 target* want to watch past the *skip ad* button five seconds into the advertising.

Moving from *science* to *art* is cumbersome. Take the time to look past the beauty of your *art* and make sure to maintain the foundational *science*.

In the *Febreze* example, the brand mitigated risk by launching multiple test markets to confirm a successful translation. Many brands cannot afford this luxury. No matter how small the brand, the immediate next step should validate whether you truly found the *opportunity among the chaos.*

SIX SELL A LITTLE, LEARN A LOT

The 80/20 of Marketing Activation

Use only that which works, and take it from any place you can find it.

\- *Bruce Lee*

You have analyzed the data and crafted the message. Now it is time to see how well your brand will motivate the *80/20 target*. At this point, marketing success hinges on the plan.

Procter & Gamble creates marketing plans in a carefully structured manner. Every element of the marketing plan is deliberate and supports a higher-level purpose. The consistently productive tool Procter & Gamble uses is the *OGSM* strategic planning process attributed to the Japanese

automobile manufacturers during the post-World
War II recovery.

OGSM

OGSM is an acronym for *objective, goal, strategies*,
and *measures.* We never discussed a specific marketing tactic without first considering how that
tactic fit into the ultimate *objective.* Here is how
we defined the elements of *OGSM*:

- *Objective* – We introduced the *marketing
  objective* in the last chapter. The *objective*
  is what the marketing initiative should
  accomplish. Recall the *objective* will most
  likely be *awareness, trial,* or *repeat.* In our
  Warby Parker example, the *objective* would
  be *trial* since many respondents heard of
  Warby Parker, but only a few had purchased the brand.
- *Goal* – The *goal* is how we quantify the *objective.* If the *Warby Parker objective* is *trial*,
  we must define success. For example, the
  marketing plan *goal* would be to increase
  trial from 15% to 25% or sell 10,000 incremental units to first-time buyers. This
  numeric value allows us to precisely assess whether the marketing effort was ultimately successful or not.
- *Strategies* – The *strategies* are the building
  blocks for delivering the *objective.* Procter & Gamble marketing plans are likely

to have three *strategies*. Continuing with the *Warby Parker* example, those *strategies* might be increased optical care distribution, couponing, and virtual style match.

- *Measures* – Similar to the *goal*, *measures* are how the *strategies* are quantified. Example *measures* might be increasing optical care distribution from 30% to 50%, two-thousand coupon redemptions, and ten-thousand virtual eyewear website impressions.

At any point after launch, we were able to assess our progress by tracking our *goal* and monitoring the *measures* to understand which *strategies* contributed most. Tactical brainstorms worked well in this structure. Divergent ideas from these brainstorms were quickly separated into the *strategic* buckets or eliminated if not aligned to a *strategy*.

FROM PLAN TO ACTION

My first full-time role at Procter & Gamble was as an assistant brand manager in Juice New Global Development. This group was not in support of existing Procter & Gamble brands. It was charged with creating new brands. In this environment, one where the vast majority of initiatives fail, I was trained to mitigate launch risks. We did this by following a mantra of *sell a little, learn a lot*. This idea manifested most frequently in the form of test markets, but we did this in a more granular manner in New Business Development. The salesperson and I personally stocked a few locally owned businesses to see how shoppers reacted to our new product. The agreement was that the local stores would keep any revenue for units sold, but they agreed to share the sales data. We were also allowed to sample in the store and glean insight from shopper interactions.

As we learned and implemented from that small local test, we introduced the product to the Procter & Gamble store. This store was for employees only and payment was with P&G dollars employees earned through volunteering as consumer testers on other company products. The Procter & Gamble store tracking was more detailed than the local test because it tracked more than overall sales. The store gathered data on whether a sale was a *trial*, whether a sale was a *repeat* purchase, and, for *repeat* purchases, time from last purchase and number of *repeats*.

Sources of data were abundant at Procter & Gamble. Fortunately, technology has caught up and given everyone a similar advantage. Digital marketing has different, but just as useful, metrics to verify if your marketing plan is on the right track. This marketing vehicle is attractive to brands of all sizes. Unlike traditional media, with digital marketing, you can begin advertising with no money down and set daily marketing spend limits as low as a few dollars a day.

BRINGING SCIENCE TO THE ART

When creating your marketing plan, you take consumer data (the *science*) and craft it into a hopefully compelling message (the *art*). With digital marketing, you can bring *science* back into the evaluation of the *art*. You can measure how a message performs with your *80/20 target* in a sample size that is statistically significant. This ability has been revolutionary for my marketing clients in understanding consumer preferences and messaging improvements. Clients have witnessed how different messages have performed on *Facebook*, *Google*, *LinkedIn*, and *Twitter*. Although I believe they trust my judgment, the recommendations are especially persuasive when the data analysis is on my side.

In the spirit of 80/20, I will not attempt to teach all there is to know about digital marketing. Instead, I suggest that 80% of the benefit may be realized by understanding four terms.

  - *Clicks* – Assuming a constant budget, the mouse *click* is a metric that helps you understand marketing campaign effectiveness. Getting our *80/20 target* to *click* on a link is what we design the advertisement to elicit. The more *clicks* we attract, the closer we theoretically get to meeting our *marketing objective.*

- *Click-Through Rate (CTR)* – *Click-through rate* is a measure of how many impressions it takes for your target to *click*. The fewer advertising impressions necessary for a *click*, the more *engaging* your message. *Engagingness* helps us understand how well the message breaks through the clutter.

- *Cost per Click (CPC)* – *Cost per click* is how much you pay every time someone *clicks* your ad. The less you spend, the more cost efficiency your ad. Variations in *CPC* are predominantly a function of differences in target popularity and geographic scope. The more brands that are interested in a specific target, the more it will cost to deliver advertising impressions to this target. Geographically, you will find targeting the United States is less expensive than targeting the state of Georgia because you have a larger pool of users that might *click* your advertisement. Digital marketing platforms have algorithms that will find less targeted, and therefore less expensive, populations. *Cost per thousand impressions (CPM)* is another metric for cost efficiency.

- *Conversions* – A *conversion* is the most important metric because it connects digital with actual. Examples of *conversions* might be a purchase, a test drive, an in-store visit, or an email share. Consider *conversions* to be the *moment of truth* that shows success with the *80/20 target*. Unlike the other digital metrics described, *conversions* are not automatically collected. We must consciously integrate *conversions* into the digital marketing effort.

The rich data delivered from digital marketing makes it an invaluable tool for most marketing executions. Since beginning my work as a marketing consultant, I have never led a marketing execution that did not start with digital marketing. In addition to yielding value as a marketing vehicle, the metric-based aspect of digital marketing provides consumer research value. Brand builders can validate marketing *messages*, *80/20 targets*, and other variables in a basic digital marketing test. A motivated Georgia Tech undergraduate student discovered this for himself working with a local Atlanta brand.

80/20 BRAND EXPERIMENT

At the beginning of the Fall 2017 semester, an undergraduate student called to request my supervision on an independent study. This request was not usual. Past independent studies involved graduate students who had a clear vision of what they wanted to learn. In his last semester before graduating, this student simply knew that he was interested in learning more about brand management.

I agreed to move forward with his independent study on two conditions. The first condition was that he would work with the same brand his group analyzed when he took my Strategic Brand Management class. The second condition was that the brand, a local cider brewery, would agree to invest a few hundred dollars to fund a digital marketing test. The student met both conditions, and we began the independent study.

In general, we wanted to learn how well one semester of the *80/20 Brand* learning approach compared to the brand building efforts of industry people who worked in the job for years. This student was part of a group that recommended that the local brewery select a different *80/20 target* and use a different marketing message. The recommendations used in the test were the same as his group presented in class in the Fall 2016 semester. Neither the *80/20 target* nor the marketing *message* was altered from the original presentation, and therefore this test did not benefit from my in-class feedback.

To execute this test we used *Facebook*, a marketing vehicle the brewery was already using. We ran four legs for up to a week with a budget of $64 for each:

- *Leg 1: Existing target with the existing message*
- *Leg 2: Existing target with the student message*
- *Leg 3: Student target with the existing message*
- *Leg 4: Student target with the student message*

The existing target was men and women between 23 and 51 years of age who drank alcohol and lived within twenty-five miles of the brewery. The students recommended a more liberal subset of that target that was more likely to be college students, more likely to attend live events, and might be considered foodies. Demographically this target was more female, more ethnically diverse, and younger: between 21 and 40 years of age.

The existing message was *From Grove to Glass* and showed a picture of an apple orchid with Atlanta in the background. It had a soft and natural feel.

The student message was *A Unique Taste of Atlanta* and showed three flavors of bottled cider. This ad attempted to highlight the various cider flavor options. In the class analysis, the students determined that *flavor* was the brand's *POD*.

The brewery defined the *marketing objective* as *drive more traffic*, which is a variation of *trial*. To better measure this *objective* we created a *conversion*. The way this *conversion* worked was that if a *Facebook* user *clicked* on an ad from any of the legs, the ad redirected the user to a page on the brewery website associated explicitly with that leg. On each page was the same call to action. The brewery agreed to offer a free tour and tasting with a printout of the page. Based on the code at the bottom of the page redeemed, we were able to track which advertisement drove the brewery visit.

Note that the bigger the budget and the longer the time period, the more statistically significant

the test results. Given the reach, we gained dir-
ectional insight (see chart below). In the control leg with the existing message and existing
target, the $64 budget reached over ninety-five
hundred *Facebook* users and ultimately delivered
two *conversions*. In each of the two subsequent
legs which switched out either the existing target
with the student target or the existing message
with the student message, there were four *conversions*. Even partial implementation of the student recommendation doubled *conversions* over
the control campaign. In the last leg, using both
the student target and the student message, there
were six *conversions*, a full three times the rate of
the control campaign.

Target	Message	Reach	Clicks	CTR	CPC	Conversions	Conversions per click
Existing	Existing	9,576	19	0.15%	$3.37	2	10.5%
Existing	Student	13,631	24	0.12%	$2.67	4	16.7%
Student	Existing	15,366	22	0.11%	$2.90	4	18.8%
Student	Student	16,631	27	0.12%	$2.37	6	22.2%

*Test spend was $64 per leg

This real-world test was the one time out of dozens of class brand consulting projects that we had
an opportunity to test the student recommendation versus an existing brand campaign. Someone
might argue that if this happened with another
brand project, the results might not have been so
flattering. Possibly, but the point of the independent study was to validate the ability of under-

graduate students to compete in a brand building environment after learning the *80/20 Brand* methodology. The undergraduate group demonstrated itself to be at the very least competent.

The broader takeaway from this experiment is that digital marketing is an important validation tool for brands with smaller budgets. We covered the fundamentals of *messaging*, but even if you feel wonderful about what you plan to communicate, it is quick and easy to test your proposed brand *message* against an alternate *message*. Digital marketing is a platform that will help you hone your marketing *message*, and sometimes your *80/20 target*, over time.

Decision making is integral to brand building. Whenever feasible, allow data from vehicles like digital marketing to provide an objective context for those decisions. Where it gets tricky is when it comes to the ultimate consumer decision. The consumer decision to buy is where we learn the strength of our efforts.

SEVEN FIRST MOMENT OF TRUTH

The 80/20 of Shopper Purchase

A moment of choice is a moment of truth.

- *Stephen Covey*

Sometimes you do everything right. You perform insightful analysis, create *engaging* advertising, and build a thoughtful marketing plan, yet the expected results do not follow. There could be many reasons for disappointing results, but Procter & Gamble suspected a frequent cause. This cause was the *First Moment of Truth* (*FMOT*) and P&G made addressing this issue a corporate priority in the early 2000s.

The call to address the *First Moment of Truth* issue was led by former Procter & Gamble CEO, A. G.

Lafley. The premise was that a consumer might tell us something about preferences or buying habits, but we could see the truth when the consumer voted with her dollars. From this premise, Lafley identified two *moments of truth*. The *First Moment of Truth* was whether a shopper selected your brand in the store and purchased it. The *Second Moment of Truth* was when she experienced the product and, based on that experience, decided whether she would buy it again.

With a heavy emphasis on Product Development, Procter & Gamble did well when it came to the *Second Moment of Truth*. However, if we did not win at the *First Moment of Truth*, the consumer could not consider us in the *Second Moment of Truth*. According to our Consumer Knowledge function around 75% to 80% of purchase decisions are made in-store increasing the urgency for a *First Moment of Truth* solution.

CAFÉ LATTE

The *First Moment of Truth* was a struggle for many of us. As a new assistant brand manager on the *Folgers* brand, I was responsible for a recently launched brand extension intended to connect with a younger consumer. It was a frothy, flavored coffee that appealed to a more youthful palate called *Folgers Café Latte*. This initiative performed well in the test market but was below projections in the national launch. The data was perplexing.

Our *awareness* and *repeat* were in line with expectations, but our *trial* was significantly below forecasts. *Awareness*, as we mentioned earlier, was directly affected by the media weight. *Repeat* was driven by how well the product performed: the *Second Moment of Truth*. What could be hurting our *trial*?

This question perplexed the *Folgers* brand, and when I took over the initiative, I had no quick solution. While pouring through the data and working with the cross-functional *Café Latte* team, I received a call from our customer support group. A shopper had seen our television commercial and, motivated by the advertising, went to her nearest *Kroger* to purchase the product. Thankfully, this shopper took the time to call the brand and let us know that we were sold out in her local grocery store. Hearing that we sold out in a store was encouraging but did not align with the data. I reached out to our Sales manager and asked him to visit the store. If this shopper was correct, we needed to restock quickly and make sure we stayed in stock.

I was not surprised to hear from our Sales manager that we were, to the contrary, fully stocked with *Café Latte* in that specific *Kroger*. In this situation, shopper *trial* was hampered by the *First Moment of Truth*.

The segment of creamy, frothy coffees was not

new. Products in this segment were most commonly identified by a foamy picture of coffee on the package. *Café Latte* did not have a picture and shoppers who were actively looking for this offering simply did not see it. We worked with our creative agency to create an updated package that included a frothy coffee image. A simple change that overwhelmingly solved the *First Moment of Truth* issue in our subsequent shopper testing.

Encouraged by this shopper validated success, I pitched this simple change through the Procter & Gamble approval chain to reverse the issue. The brand manager was on board. The marketing director also supported this change. Unfortunately, we hit a glitch with the coffee category general manager. He was an Operations veteran who was reluctant to discard the existing packaging label inventory to improve shelf presence. The unwillingness to make the packaging upgrade until we exhausted label inventory led to the failure of the *Café Latte* initiative.

As I returned to my desk after an unsuccessful meeting with the coffee category general manager, I ran into the category Finance manager and shared our proposed package change. Ironically, she mentioned that we had a picture of creamy, frothy coffee on the package in the test market. The creamy coffee image was reportedly removed before launch to create a more consistent *Folgers* brand block. The difference between the test market and national results immediately made sense. Fortunately, we reapplied this critical learning to a similar effort called *Folgers Cappuccino* that continues to this day.

Examples like this across Procter & Gamble led to the newly created role of First Moment of Truth brand manager. Ironically, the *Café Latte* initiative failure was a positive experience when seeking promotion into this role.

FMOT FRAMEWORK

As we looked into the specific causes for poor *First Moment of Truth* performance, we identified many *purchase barriers*, but two *barriers* surfaced more than others:

- *Consideration Set* – Shoppers tend to enter stores with a good idea of what to purchase. This is typically a specific version of a product from a subset of brands. Version includes type, flavor, scent, size, and other designations that shoppers use to identify the option they seek. Products that meet the version and brand requirements comprise the set of options the shopper considers. *Café Latte* suffered from a common *consideration set* issue called *findability.* Shoppers searched for a particular item but did not find it. In other situations, products do not make the *consideration set* because shoppers simply fail to notice a product that would meet predefined requirements when considering options.

- *Value* – Sometimes we see a commercial of a product that appears to address an *accepted consumer belief*, but when we get to the store shelf the product does not exude the same convincingness of the advertisement. When in doubt, the default option is to do without. Other times, the product may convince a shopper but happens to be near *competitors* that appear to deliver a more significant benefit. Price is always a consideration. When a shopper perceives multiple products to be similar, the default choice is the cheapest one. Rather than winning the low-price battle, seek ways to reframe *value*. To help address *value* perception, Eric Almquist, John Senior, and Nicolas Bloch wrote an article titled *The Elements of Value* detailing thirty elements of *value* organized in the buckets of functional, emotional, life changing and social impact. To address the *value purchase barrier*, we will focus on the first two buckets.

- *Functional value* – According to *The Elements of Value*, *functional value* has fourteen elements. The most common of those elements used at the *First Moment of Truth* from my experience are *saves time, simplifies, reduces risk, reduces effort, avoids hassles, reduces cost*, and *quality*. The *Bounty* paper towel package advertises the *Select-A-Size*, a form of *reduces cost* because of the ability to use only what is needed, while the *2x more absorbent* claim is a form of *reduces effort* because more mess may be cleaned with fewer wipes.

- *Emotional value* – The most commonly used of the ten emotional elements at the *First Moment of Truth* are *rewards me, badge value, fun*, and *attractiveness*. When Coca-Cola launched the *Share a Coke* campaign featuring common first names, the brand was able to build *emotional value* by leveraging the *fun* element.

As previously demonstrated in the *Folgers Café*

Latte example, product packaging is a critical element of the *First Moment of Truth*. There are many in-store marketing vehicle options, but brand builders are at the mercy of individual stores for correct implementation, and some retailers with a clean store policy ban many of the most attention-grabbing options. We decided that the 80/20 for the *First Moment of Truth* was powerful package messaging because marketers have control of the package design.

Aligned on this priority, I led an initiative to improve Procter & Gamble package messaging following a framework similar to the one below:

- *Identification (ID)* – Includes brand elements, such as brand name, logo, colors, fonts, and anything else that helps the shopper recognize the brand. *Coca-Cola's* font is so iconic that any name could be written on a can and you would still know it is *Coke*. Ironically, ample identification is seldom the issue with package messaging. The work in *identification* is including brand elements in a way that does not interfere with the packaging *point of parity* or *point of difference* communication. *Less is more* with this principle.
- *Point of Parity (POP)* – Recall *point of parity* in the context of *positioning*. It described options a consumer might choose if your brand was not available. Similarly, pack-

age messaging *Point of Parity* communicates what is necessary for inclusion in the shopper *consideration set*. The cause for the *Café Latte* initiative failure was due to the lack of a creamy, frothy coffee image. This issue of *findability* prevented *Café Latte* from being included in the shopper *consideration set*. Think of package messaging *Point of Parity* as the means for overcoming the *consideration set shopper barrier*.

- *Point of Difference* (POD) – The *point of difference* is where we address the *value purchase barrier*. When I was on *Folgers*, our *80/20 target* typically chose between *Maxwell House* and us. The purchase decision was most commonly based on which brand had a lower price on that visit. When we changed over from metal to plastic cans, our *80/20 target* became less price sensitive. We addressed *functional value* in two ways. First, we advertised plastic can conversion with a *freshness* message addressing the *quality element*. Second, the plastic material allowed us to mold handles into the side of the can creating a *reduces effort* element. In many focus group studies, we witnessed that more shoppers than expected kept empty cans after using the coffee for other household purposes. The easily reusable plastic cans reinforced an existing consumer behavior, therefore bringing *emotional value* through the *rewards me* element.

FEBREZE AND CREST EXPANSIONS

New brand initiatives used the *ID*, *POP*, *POD* framework to improve launch results and shared the successes throughout the company. The framework timing was opportune for *Febreze*. After years of solid business growth, the brand was ready to enter the aerosol air fresheners category. The plan was to enter the premium segment, priced around $2.99, against competitors such as *Oust* and *Neutra Air,* but *Febreze* was most concerned about *Glade*. *Glade's* price point was only about half that of the premium segment at around $1.39, but as the category leader *Glade* was expected to respond aggressively.

Knowing the importance of the *First Moment of Truth*, *Febreze* designed their *Air Effects* aerosol as follows:
ID: *Febreze* used the *breath of fresh air* window logo, brand name, and light blue color across the top of the spray can to alert shoppers that a brand they knew and trusted was now in the aerosol category.
POP: For inclusion in an aerosol *consideration set* the scent is a guiding attribute, so *Febreze* made the scents visually *engaging* and easy to find along the bottom of each can. Notice the scents are

more prominent than the brand name.

POD: *Febreze* addressed the *functional value purchase barrier* by leveraging the *reduces effort* element with the use of an ergonomically correct spray trigger. To create *emotional value*, *Febreze* pursued the *attractiveness* element. The brand introduced a distinctive category can shape to create a futuristic look.

As expected, the *Febreze Air Effects* launch suffered aggressive competitive response, but the brand's *First Moment of Truth* efforts were rewarded with results that were significantly above expectations. Revenue was 80% above projection, volume was 78% above projection, and *repeat* rate was 37% above projection.

Coming off the success of *Whitestrips*, *Crest* was beaten to the premium toothpaste market segment by *Colgate*. *Colgate's* premium tier offering touted a whitening benefit superior to existing whitening toothpastes, but at a price far below that of *Crest Whitestrips*. This profitable toothpaste segment was growing quickly to the benefit of *Colgate*. Like *Febreze*, *Crest* knew that *First Moment of Truth* would be an advantage the brand would need given its late entry. Here is how *Crest* approached package messaging:

ID: Recall that *less is more* when it comes to *identification*. This minimalism is also the case with premium items. *Crest* used a modest logo, allowing the blue brand color to carry most of the *equity identity* weight.

POP: *Colgate* set the tone for shopper expectations in this segment and *Crest* followed suit. The package orientation was vertical rather than horizontal, and the benefit communication focused on whitening.

POD: *Crest* concentrated on the *attractiveness element* in hopes of addressing the *emotional value purchase barrier*. The Marketing function convinced Operations to invest more in *First Moment of Truth* by agreeing to allocate a portion of packaging cost to the marketing budget. This budget allowed high-tier beauty cues, such as embossing and foil creating a premium look.

Once again, the *First Moment of Truth* gamble paid off. *Crest Vivid White* reached parity share with *Colgate Simply White* in the segment within six weeks of launch. Even more encouraging was the fact that *Crest Vivid White* exceeded the sales forecast by nearly 300%!

While the examples we illustrated in this chapter were with consumer products in retail outlets, the *First Moment of Truth* is not limited to this realm. Similar dynamics exist with services and online retailers. The key to success is figuring out how to overcome the *purchase barriers* of *consideration set* and *value* regardless of offering type and shopper interface.

We did not detail all thirty elements of *value* from the *Harvard Business Review* article by Almquist, Senior, and Bloch, but one *value* element deserves more in-depth exploration. According to these *Bain & Company* strategists, *Some elements do matter more than others. Across all the industries we studied, perceived quality affects customer advocacy more than any other element. Products and services must attain a certain minimum level, and no other elements can make up for a significant shortfall on this one.*

We should not overlook this finding. *No value* element is more important than *perceived quality*. No one will argue with the importance of *quality*. At price parity, the rational shopper chooses the highest *quality*. Or does she?

EIGHT PRODUCT PLACEBO

The 80/20 of Quality Perception

This is not just making it up in your mind. The placebo effect has a biology. The pathways that we know the placebo effects use are the pathways many significant drugs use.

\-   *Ted J. Kaptchuk*

When describing *point of difference* for the *First Moment of Truth*, we used the *Folgers* plastic can transition example. Something I did not mention earlier is that *Maxwell House* responded with a radio advertisement explaining that metal cans keep coffee fresher than plastic cans, in direct contradiction to the *Folgers* freshness message. I never saw any data on this, but *Maxwell House* may have been correct. The takeaway is that the data was not nearly as compelling as the ingrained association consumers had with the *Tupperware* brand. *Tupperware* trained us that we keep food fresh in plastic containers. This association motivated shopper behavior. *Maxwell House* relented and followed *Folgers* by also introducing plastic cans.

We used the *Febreze* messaging example to illustrate how small nuances in communication can be the difference between the success and failure of an initiative. Although the difference in *message* effectiveness seemed to be caused by something as minor as word choice, it is connected to something more profound. The consumer response to *traps odor* versus *cleans odor* exposes a quirk in how human beings are wired.

MOUTHWASH AND KNEE SURGERY

Every semester I show my classes a picture of *Crest Pro-Health* mouthwash next to a bottle of *Listerine*. I ask them which mouthwash they would choose assuming the same size and price. Recognizing that both brands kill the germs that cause bad breath, the majority of students consistently select *Listerine*. When I ask the students why *Listerine*, they list logical reasons like *Listerine's* focus in the mouthwash segment. I might hear that this is the brand their family has used for years. Eventually, someone says he or she likes *Listerine* because it burns. That's right. The student prefers *Listerine* to *Crest Pro-Health*, not because it kills bacteria better or any other claim *Listerine* makes. The student likes *Listerine* because it hurts. Yes, an otherwise negative characteristic is the reason for purchase. The pain is the *point of difference*.

Understanding that both brands deliver the segment benefit of fresh breath, the burning sensation serves as a confirmation of benefit delivery. Mouthwash technology has advanced to the point where burning is not necessary for efficacy yet burning is essential from a perceptual standpoint.
  Remember that Almquist, Senior, and Bloch learned that no *value* element is more important than *perceived quality*.

This psychological advantage plays out over and over again in different consumer situations. It even plays out in areas as serious as medicine. If a doctor instructs patients to take pills to address a given illness, some percentage will experience improvements even if those pills contain no medicine. This phenomenon is known as the placebo effect.

The placebo effect is a widely recognized factor in medicine that is one of the standard control methods the Federal Drug Administration outlines in their *Guidance for Institutional Review Boards and Clinical Investigators*; the process necessary to validate new drug effectiveness before a

AARON HACKETT

company may market it.

A ritual that is thought to deliver an expected outcome works, even when it should not. To test the extent of the placebo effect, a professor at *Harvard Medical School* tested the responses after giving patients suffering from irritable bowel syndrome an open-label placebo or nothing. An open-label placebo is when the doctor tells the patient that what he or she is getting is only a placebo and nothing more. The patients who were told they were getting a placebo had significantly improved symptoms to their irritable bowel syndrome versus the patients who received nothing. Even when a patient knows he or she is getting a placebo, it works, emphasizing the magnitude of this wonder. Moreover, the placebo effect in the medical field goes well beyond pills.

In July of 2002, the *New England Journal of Medicine* published a study that tested the placebo effect in knee surgery. Patients in this double-blind test with knee osteoarthritis received either the actual knee surgery or merely had the skin on their knee cut open with doctors acting like they performed the surgery. The results of this controlled trial were that patients that received surgery had similar levels of pain relief than the patients who only had their knee cut open but with no surgery. The conclusion from this study reads, *In this controlled trial involving patients with osteoarthritis of the knee, the outcomes after arthroscopic lavage or arthroscopic débridement were no better than those after a placebo procedure.*

This compelling dynamic illustrates the power of the mind. In our *Costco* example, we demonstrated the strength of the *Huggies brand equity* over that of *Kirkland Signature* with the 30% price premium on virtually the same diaper. *Huggies* primarily developed this advantage through advertising, the most pervasive method of building *brand equity*. This works, but advertising can expensive. What if we could alter the consumer experience to build a similar level of loyalty for a fraction of the cost?

Product placebos are less commonly used, yet exceptionally effective in building *brand equity*. Recognizing this opportunity for improved consumer experience, as brand builders, it is our responsibility to leverage placebos when reasonably possible to deepen brand relationships with the *80/20 target*.

PLACEBO UPGRADE

Before I began teaching, I worked as the vice president of marketing and general manager for a private equity company based in Alpharetta, Georgia. In one of my categories, I noticed an odd dynamic. Two laundry products had consumer perceptions that were the opposite of our Research and Development findings. Consumers loved one product, but our Research and Development team could not find measurable differences in performance versus plain tap water during testing. The brand equity in this situation seemed to deliver the perception. With the other product, *Dryel*, the Research and Development team was able to confirm that it killed significant levels of bacteria on clothing, yet consumers were skeptical. Lab-confirmed performance that does not translate into a consumer-noticeable benefit is a glaring sign that a placebo would be helpful.

Dryel is an at-home dry cleaning product launched by Procter & Gamble in 1999 and later purchased by the Alpharetta based private equity firm. The product was designed for use with a typical home dryer and included a dryer bag and steam cleaning cloths. Users placed these cleaning cloths in the *Dryel* bag with the clothes to be dry cleaned and tumbled the bag in the dryer on the normal setting. Before launch, the concept of caring for *dry clean only* clothes at home was compelling. Consumers loved it, but the experience did not meet consumer expectations in a couple of areas.

Consumers compared the *Dryel* experience to their experiences with local dry cleaners. When consumers picked up clothes from the dry cleaner, they were neatly hung and pressed. When pulling clothes from the *Dryel* bag, they were slightly wrinkled. The other, more critical perceptual issue was cleaning efficacy. Clothes came out with a fresh, clean scent, but I was aware of consumer feedback that questioned whether the scent merely masked clothing odors.

Given the magnitude of the issue, it made sense to ask for guidance. We traveled to Cincinnati to speak with the Research and Development person credited with the brand launch. Using the reams of shopper data the team collected at the Procter & Gamble store, she determined that a couple of clothing articles had an unusually high correlation with *repeat* purchase. Those clothing articles were sweaters and jeans. In retrospect, it made sense. Sweaters and jeans do not have the same pressing requirements as other dry clean clothing. Instead of pressing, Dryel offered a more meaningful benefit. The coveted benefit was keeping clothes like new. The benefit indicator for sweaters was shape retention, and for jeans was color retention. Testing for both benefits showed Dryel to deliver these results significantly better than regular washing.

Addressing cleaning perception was more complicated. We looked to notable product placebo examples to improve *Dryel*, first returning to the *Listerine* placebo. Recall the burning sensation of *Listerine* delivering the cleaning perception. Similarly, we dialed down the fresh, clean scent and added an alcohol top note to produce a clinical, rather than floral, sensation.

Next, we looked to the *Betty Crocker* placebo. The *Betty Crocker* story is regarding the cake mix. When the cake mix was launched it delivered the ultimate convenience with a great taste. Moms only needed to add water to the mix, which included all the ingredients, and bake for a delicious cake. Even with this groundbreaking innovation, the sales were disappointing. It took an Austrian consumer psychologist to pinpoint the problem. It was guilt. His theory was that moms did not feel like the effort they exerted allowed them to claim that they indeed made the cakes, and sales remained flat over time. *Betty Crocker* researched the issue and reformulated the product requiring moms to add an egg, in addition to water. That simple adjustment added enough complexity and mess to deliver a more homemade, yet convenient, cooking experience and sales grew.

The *Betty Crocker* placebo parallel for *Dryel* was adding cleaning fluid in spray bottle form. Previously, the cleaning agent was limited to the cleaning cloth. By adding a small spray bottle of cleaning agent, we allowed users to apply more cleaning solution to areas of clothing that might specifically require more attention, significantly improving actual cleaning, and more importantly, perceived cleaning. The extra work undoubtedly translated into an improved consumer experience.

Finally, we explored the *Tide* placebo. As clothing washing technology improved, Product Development recognized that the bubble production we see in the washing machine was an inefficient by-product of the cleaning process. Therefore, Product Development reformulated *Tide* to clean without the superfluous bubbles. It did not take long for the customer support lines to light up. The absence of bubbles led to the perception that the detergent was not working. *Tide* quickly learned that those superfluous bubbles had a vital placebo effect.

Our Research and Development team explored how users might see evidence of cleansing on the cleaning cloths to create the *Tide* placebo effect in the *Dryel* product. This evidence would allow us to surpass cleaning perception issues without question. The team worked to find a way to show the dirt on used cleaning cloths, but with no success. Although we were not able to implement the *Tide* placebo on *Dryel*, I share the thinking to demonstrate the multidimensional approach of using placebos to improve consumer perceptions.

When a brand implements product placebos, it is an opportune time to investigate other areas of potential improvement to build a synergistic effect. We looked at a couple of areas.

Product placebos are generally helpful with *repeat*. *Trial* was also an issue, and *Dryel* had work to do in the *First Moment of Truth* area. During store checks, company employees reported a problem with *findability*. They would walk right by it. To better convey clean, the *Dryel* package color was off-white, a color not that different from many store shelves. As we explored the right color to help *Dryel* stand out on the shelf, the president of the company, Tom Penner, offhandedly suggested we use black. Penner pointed to the highly successful launch of *U by Kotex* in feminine hygiene as an example of how black might work in a category known for lighter colors.

The *Dryel* team brought a black package mockup to shopper research, along with a safer lavender package option. In addition to the two colors, we included a side cutout so that shoppers could easily see the newly added spray bottle designed to deliver the *Betty Crocker* placebo. Both options tested better than the current off-white packaging, but black had greater shelf stopping power and elicited more passion from shoppers.

As part of our research protocol, we also used the shopper interaction to refine verbiage and probe for additional areas of improvement. The shopper groups provided surprising feedback. What *Dryel* thought of as part of the design equity carried no consumer value. On the contrary, consumers found this element to be confusing. The design element was the steam swirl, meant to convey gentle cleaning. Instead, consumers mistook the steam for water which had no place in the *Dryel* cleaning process. *Dryel* had too much *identification* at the *First Moment of Truth*. We pulled that element and replaced it with a picture of a woman wearing jeans and a sweater, a head nod to the clothes that performed best with *Dryel*. In the spirit of transparency, our creative director decided to serve as the model on the package and did an excellent job.

The other area we improved was *messaging*. Contrary to the 80/20 rule, the older *Dryel* package boldly claimed, *Now for use on ALL your Clothes!* in the top right corner. While someone may use *Dryel* on all of her clothes, the performance would not be superior, or even comparable, to regular machine washing on most items. This *all clothes* claim was an attempt at driving usage occasions that had little credibility. We needed to get focused, similar to how we honed-in on the travel occasion for *Downy Wrinkle Releaser*. From the Cincinnati visit, we established that jeans and sweaters were our hero clothing items. Just as we showcased them on the new packaging, we needed to leverage our *keep clothes like new point of difference* in our advertising.

Even after identifying two hero clothing items, we did not water down our message by trying to advertise both in the same communication. We dedicated one advertisement to jeans and the other ad to sweaters. Both items shared the *accepted consumer belief*, a desire to keep clothes like new, but the executions were individual.

Jeans ad:
- *Jeans headline - Dryel.* Keep your dark jeans dark.
- *Jeans image* - Woman wearing jeans that look dark and new.
- *Jeans reason to believe* - Visual representation of jeans washed ten times in detergent versus jeans cleaned fifty times with *Dryel*.

Sweater ad:
- *Sweater headline - Dryel.* Keep your sweater in shape. No shrinking and No stretching.
- *Sweater image* - Woman wearing a fitted sweater.
- *Sweater reason to believe* - Visual representation of a sweater washed five times in detergent versus a sweater cleaned five times with *Dryel*.

The resulting *Dryel* product and messaging improvements delivered increased consumer satisfaction and allowed the brand to continue sales growth in the face of a significantly reduced marketing budget. The calculation is straightforward. A *product placebo* increases *quality* perception, which in turn improves the consumer experience. This improved experience, or *Second Moment of Truth*, increases the likelihood of *repeat*, and ultimately loyalty.

SERVICE PLACEBO

The chapter is called *Product Placebo*, but this dynamic is just as relevant in services. For example, when I was on the *Folgers* brand, we attributed the meteoric rise of *Starbucks* to the in-store experience more than the product. Many other service brands may come to mind, but let us revisit the medical field, our starting place for discussing placebos.

According to a study published by the *Journal of the American Medical Association*, when it comes to malpractice lawsuits, how primary care physicians talk about diagnoses or treatments mattered as much as the diagnoses or treatments themselves. Primary care physicians significantly lowered their risks of malpractice suits by outlining expectations for patients, encouraging patient feedback, and even laughing more in visits. The primary care physicians with no malpractice lawsuits spent about three minutes more with patients during visits than those with two or more lawsuits. Physicians with a *personality placebo* have a lower legal risk.

I chose *Product Placebo* as the last chapter of this book because it is a deceptively powerful yet overlooked brand building tool. The influence of placebos parallels the *brand equity* advantage of leading brands over generic products. Placebos deliver their benefit, not necessarily in a rational way, but more persuasively, through firmly held consumer beliefs. These beliefs allow the connection to go beyond analytical to emotional. Emotionally connecting to the *80/20 target* is the ultimate path to building meaningful brands. Go for consumer experience over brand explanation.

THE EIGHTY PERCENT

There is no question that other experienced brand builders will challenge the twenty percent of the brand fundamentals that deliver eighty percent of the results. This varied perspective will remain an area of debate and, with advances in marketing, will undoubtedly evolve. I have come to the twenty percent in this book by evaluating brand building from three different perspectives, each backed by many years of experience: brand manager, brand consultant, and brand professor.

This final section is an acknowledgment of some of the areas that might arise for debate. I have worked with, and taught, each of these areas in the past. If you have a desire to expand beyond the twenty percent, these are intriguing areas to explore. Building competence in the twenty percent in this book before that exploration will make the learning in those areas exceedingly more enlightening.

Design elements and development – Design elements such as the logo, brand colors, brand characters, and brand names are fundamental. Design elements, outside of our discussion on packaging, were not covered in this book for a couple of reasons. The first is that creative agencies typically create brand elements, although brand builders manage the process by providing strategic direction. The other reason is that in the vast majority of situations, a brand builder does not make changes to the brand elements.

Creative design is a different skill set that is rarely mastered by brand builders. Although we might decide to unleash our creative side, hiring a creative agency is a prudent decision. Becoming proficient in design is a different objective than becoming skilled in brand building. For those brand builders in a position to create brand elements, I will share this word of advice. Put a disproportionate effort into selecting the brand name. This element is the hardest to change later in the life of a brand. When choosing a brand name in this web-based environment, you must consider your ability to secure the web address in parallel with selecting the brand name. Specifically, get the dot-com address. For web addresses, a shorter name is better. Numbers and special characters can also be problematic in web addresses.

Borrowing brand equity – Co-branding, licensing, and celebrity endorsements are a few ways to borrow *brand equity* from other entities. This method of brand building is useful in many situations. The focus of this book is to build *brand equity* without the help of this shortcut. If you can build equity independently, borrowing equity will only fuel your momentum. The best way to experiment with borrowing *brand equity* is in the brand activation stage, especially using digital marketing to validate the value of a partner.

Extending a brand – Brand extension is a natural form of growth. There are specific areas of focus in launching extensions, but the priority for this book was to show how to build an existing brand recognizing that this knowledge would carry over to brand extensions. Flavor, size, or even line extensions, are pretty routine for a knowledgeable brand builder. The strategic horsepower is required when considering extending a brand into other segments or categories.

When we discussed brand *positioning* in *Less is More*, we started with the brand *point of difference* and then defined the *80/20 target* by identifying who would find the most value in this *point of difference*. When extending the brand into new segments or categories, the starting point becomes the *80/20 target*. Determine how to meet the needs of the *80/20 target* better than the *competition* in the new area. Think about how the brand *point of difference* translates to this new area and how well it reinforces existing *brand equity*. Of course, the operational intricacies require careful consideration.

There are many more areas of brand management to explore, such as brand portfolio management and brand architecture, but rather than diverging into the various other brand areas, consider converging. The tough strategic work is getting to the core of what delivers the greatest success in the most efficient manner possible.

Brand building doesn't have to be complicated.

EPILOGUE 64/4
BRAND

The 80/20 of the 80/20

> *I've missed more than 9,000 shots in my career. I've lost almost 300 games. Twenty-six times I've been trusted to take the game winning shot and missed. I've failed over and over and over again in my life. And that is why I succeed.*
>
> - *Michael Jordan*

This book was intentionally written to be more intuitive than academic, using brand stories to help clarify concepts. Rather than pressing the memorization of concepts, the vision was for you to understand the underlying logic. The hard work of *80/20 Brand* was taking the complexities of brand management and distilling them to their simplest and most profound lessons. To reinforce the lessons shared, we will end with three salient reminders, plus one parting piece of advice.

80/20 TARGET

The *80/20 target* is the focus of chapter one. Targeting is the most fundamental marketing decision, but brands consistently shortcut this process, identifying a reasonable target rather than exerting the strategic horsepower to precisely identify the distinct target. By definition, your *80/20 target* description should be so narrowly focused that it represents about 20% of the consumer base that would be responsible for roughly 80% of brand revenue.

Settling for a reasonable target introduces a lack of precision in your marketing efforts that compounds the further you travel towards marketing execution. To reach your *80/20 target* you must go past demographics and psychographics. You must identify a specific behavior. Demographics help with visualization of the target and is useful when casting talent in advertising creative, but our increasingly diverse society no longer may be adequately targeted with only demographics.

When I facilitate the *Tom's of Maine* toothpaste case study in class, a proposed target is often moms with young kids. While reasonable, this demographic target pales in comparison to the organic food buyer. The behavior of buying organic food demonstrates a mindset that mirrors that of someone who would consider going against conventional wisdom and buying a toothpaste that does not contain fluoride. This mindset is one that is interested in reducing interactions with toxins and chemicals. Rather than convincing the mom with young kids to go against what she has believed about fluoride her entire life, you can convince an organic food buyer to extend her currently responsible behavior beyond food into another category that also happens to involve the mouth and possible toxic ingestion.

Understanding your *80/20 target* is the difference between winning and losing. If only one strategic decision garners sufficient brand attention, it should be addressing the *80/20 target*. Everything hinges on this person. The brand exists to meet this person's needs. At all costs, identify the 20% of consumers that should love you rather than settling for being thought of as better than average by everyone. Find that consumer who searches for your *point of difference*. Speak to her in a way that connects, even if it turns off everyone else. *Who* is more important than *how many*.

PRODUCT PLACEBO

Product placebo, the focus of the last chapter, is remarkably persuasive yet generally overlooked. During my career, I would hear stories of how certain product features had a psychological consumer influence, but I was never trained to look for ways to implement this placebo effect. I was led to believe that product placebos were random and brands who benefitted from them were fortunate. The more I have studied consumer behavior, the more I am convinced that we must program product placebos into the consumer experience.

In the *Tom's of Maine* toothpaste case study, I typically have a few students who have tried the brand, but only a small percentage of them continue using it. When I probe into this decision, the response tends to be a dissatisfaction with product performance. When these students respond that there is an issue with product performance, it is not because they measured the number of harmful bacteria killed or the ability of *Tom's of Maine* to prevent tartar. Instead, they are describing a feeling. They desire a *Listerine* burn. Just because the product is natural does not mean a *product placebo* is not possible. Consider *Dr. Bronner's* soap. This is a natural brand known for its *tingle*.

Move your consumer connection beyond logic to the five senses whenever possible. Once you convince your *80/20 target* to *try*, the feeling a *product placebo* elicits drives *repeat*.

OPPORTUNITY FROM CHAOS

We used *opportunity from chaos* to illustrate messaging, but this concept also captures the core of brand management. In my experience, brands have a chaotic existence. Each day brings a new challenge. Below is my structured approach to teasing out the opportunity from this chaos.

- *Analyze the data*. The data analysis is the *science* that provides a stable footing for navigating out of chaos. Thoughtful analysis can bring clarity from confusion. Finding the right pieces of information was the intent of chapter two, *Consumer is Boss*. The requisite pieces of information are the *point of difference*, the *80/20 target*, the *competitive set*, and the *point of parity*. As a brand constructs its *positioning*, the challenge makes sense and the direction in which to build a brand's *equity* becomes apparent.
- *Connect the dots*. This skill is how we transition from *science* to *art*. The ability to find obscure links benefits from a meditative level of listening. How does the data support crucial consumer insights? Is there an *accepted consumer belief* to address? Connecting the dots is where brand management problem-solving deviates from engineering problem-solving. There are many acceptable ways to connect the dots in any given situation, rather than the one way calculated in an engineering problem. Deciding on one of

many potentially viable solutions often seems arbitrary. In these situations, more senior brand leaders advised trusting my gut. The more experience you gain connecting the dots, the more reliable your gut becomes.

- *Tell the story.* Storytelling is the *art*. It is the most intrinsic obligation of a brand builder. Brand builders do the data analysis, listen to consumers, and spend most of their working days thinking about the brand. At the point of telling the story, we are tasked with winnowing all we know into a simple message. Our instinct is to hedge by advocating multiple benefits. When it comes to conveying a motivating marketing message, we need to be brazenly concise, and transparently clear. Only then is your story remembered and, more importantly, shared.

Strategy crafting is left-brain dominant, but compelling storytelling requires strength from the right-brain. This duality is the underlying challenge of brand building. We can excel in both spheres if we continue to check our story against the logical building blocks. The least creative brand builders can deliver highly effective marketing executions with data-based checks. Like any skill, this improves with time and practice.

To build a brand is to invite chaos. Brand builders

are continually putting out fires. Rather than being caught up in urgent activities, keep your eyes open for what opportunities arrive with the chaos.

EMBRACE YOUR FAILURES

We did not address the importance of failures directly in the book, but examples of failure were just as good, if not better, in illustrating our points than examples of success.

As predominantly type-A personalities, brand builders can effortlessly list their achievements in a manner that would impress most people. At Procter & Gamble, selling yourself is a part of the learning process. The story we do not tell as well is the story of our failures. Ironically, our failures are our greatest teachers.

After my internship, I returned to Procter & Gamble as an assistant brand manager working in Beverage New Business Development. With my internship experience and a newly minted MBA under my belt, I was ready for any challenge. I found it quickly. When creating a new brand, virtually all decisions are open for debate and I was caught in a cross-functional conflict. My brand manager vehemently disagreed with our Sales and Consumer Knowledge leaders on key aspects of the brand creation. I led the cross-functional team in many aspects, so I was in the awkward position of choosing sides.

As an ambitious young assistant brand manager, I chose what I believed to be the politically expedient decision of siding with my brand manager. He was the person who would lead my evaluation process and had a notable influence on my young brand career. I made sure to understand his thinking and then to demonstrate an ability to keep the team moving in his preferred direction. The Sales and Consumer Knowledge counterparts were not ecstatic, but we pushed forward with consistent progress. We agreed to disagree.

At the end of my first year, we did our annual reviews. As with my internship, my strength was *thinking & problem-solving* which I attribute to my previous structured engineering career. At Procter & Gamble, everyone had weaknesses, or opportunities as we referred to them. During my internship my opportunity was *communication*. As a former engineer, my explanations were insufficient. I was used to sharing an answer with only underlying assumptions and factors of safety. Recall, engineers only had one right answer. This review, my opportunity was *collaboration*. Given the existing conflict, this opportunity made sense. Mentors coached me that as long as my opportunities were not one of the two critical *what counts factors* (*thinking & problem-solving* or *leadership*) I was fine. Given that *thinking & problem-solving* was a strength and *leadership* did not show up as an opportunity, I was comforted concerning the feedback and my focus returned to building the business.

A couple of days later my marketing director, James Haskett, asked to speak with me. For context, brand managers reported to marketing directors. About once a quarter marketing directors reached out to the assistant brand managers in their organization to foster relationships. Assistant brand managers remained busy, but these meetings took priority. After asking how things were going and doing the customary check to make sure I had any support required, the conversation shifted to my annual review.

Haskett gently helped me understand that my annual review was not as acceptable as I had thought. Although the guidance of my mentors was correct, *collaboration,* it turns out, was a prerequisite to *leadership.* If I had an issue in *collaboration*, I would not be an effective *leader.* In a direct yet supportive manner, Haskett informed me that if I did not turn this around by my next evaluation, we would have to part ways.

For a young, motivated assistant brand manager, this realization was devastating. I had moved from the San Francisco Bay Area to Cincinnati and bought a house without a consideration that things might not work out. Fortunately, Procter & Gamble training resources were deep and the corporate commitment was sincere. I spent the following year addressing this flaw. Going forward my business loyalties were no longer swayed by political considerations and my appreciation for the experience of my cross-functional counterparts deepened.

In my next annual review, *thinking & problem-solving* was still a strength but this time I had an additional strength: *collaboration*. The profound failure I had experienced the year prior motivated me to not only become proficient in *collaboration*, but fueled my progression to the top of my class in this area. Every review since that one, *thinking & problem-solving* and *collaboration* were consistent strengths, although *collaboration* evolved. My strength in *collaboration* turned into a strength in *leadership*, as my former marketing director, James Haskett patiently persuaded me years before. *Leadership* evolved into a strength in *coaching* in support of my direct reports. My passion for *coaching* led to teaching a Brand Management class to MBA and undergraduate students at Georgia Tech. Teaching students for many years led to writing this book. Without the failure as a collaborator in my first year of brand management, I would never have been prompted to document the twenty percent of brand efforts that yield the eighty percent of brand results.

Failures have delivered the clearest lessons in my brand building journey. In a fitting acknowledgement of our last reminder, embracing failures tends to serve as a less structured way to find opportunity from chaos.

Embrace your failures. Pause and acknowledge them. Then learn and grow from them. Allow your failures to mold you into the brand building expert only you can be.

NOTES

INTRODUCTION Stanford versus Procter & Gamble

The Atlantic, *The Irrational Consumer: Why Economics Is Dead Wrong About How We Make Choices: A new paper reviews how psychology, biology, and neurology are ganging up on economics to prove that, when it comes to making decisions, people are anything but rational*, January 16, 2013 by Derek Thompson; https://www.theatlantic.com/business/archive/2013/01/the-irrational-consumer-why-economics-is-dead-wrong-about-how-we-make-choices/267255/

ONE We've got it Backward

Malcolm Gladwell, *David and Goliath: Underdogs, Misfits, and the Art of Battling Giants*, 2015.

Chris Rock's Good Hair documentary, directed by Jeff Stilson, starring Chris Rock, produced by Jenny Hunter and Kevin O'Donnell, release date January 18, 2009 at Sundance and October 9, 2009 in the United States.

Vince Hudson, Senior Vice President Global Brand Strategy and Marketing Operations, *American Express*, and former Procter & Gamble Brand Manager who launched the *Crest Whitestrips* business.

Procter & Gamble 2001 Annual Report, Making Life Better; http://www.pginvestor.com/Cache/1001181139.PDF?O=PDF&T=&Y=&D=&FID=1001181139&iid=4004124

TWO Consumer is Boss

Georgia Institute of Technology MGT6308EM Strategic Brand Management MBA class, *Warby Parker Brand Consulting Project*, by students Braddon Calloway, Steven Carriere, Robin Jenkins, Bethany Schuster, and Julia Snell, Summer 2018.

THREE Less is More

Robert Browning, *Andrea del Sarto.*

Jean Paul Plumez, President and Founder, *Leadership on Paper*; https://www.lopprogram.com

Iyengar, S. S., & Lepper, M. R. (2000). *When choice is demotivating: Can one desire too much of a good thing?* Journal of Personality and Social Psychology, 79(6), 995-1006; http://dx.doi.org/10.1037/0022-3514.79.6.995

Tom's of Maine website https://www.tomsofmaine.com/

The Associated Press, *Colgate Buys Tom's Of Maine For $100M*, March 21, 2006 by Melissa McNamara; https://www.cbsnews.com/news/colgate-buys-toms-of-maine-for-100m

Huffington Post Canada, *Pampers' Mother's Day Ad Was A Gentle Nod To New Motherhood*, May 15, 2017 by Rebecca Zamon; https://www.huffingtonpost.ca/2017/05/15/pampers-mothers-day-ad_n_16622092.html

Adweek, *Ad of the Day: Luvs, Breastfeeding in public? It's a snap for Luvs moms, who simply do everything better*, September 28, 2012 by Tim Nudd; https://www.adweek.com/brand-marketing/ad-day-luvs-144053

Keller, K. L. Strategic, *Brand Management: Building, Measuring, and Managing Brand Equity*, 4th Edition, Prentice Hall Publishers, ISBN-10: 0132664259, 2012.

Peter Thiel with Blake Masters, *Zero to One: Notes on Startups, or How to Build the Future*, 2014.

Wall Street Journal, *A Costco Brand Shakes Up Rivals*, September 11, 2017 by Sarah Nassauer; https://www.foxbusiness.com/features/a-costco-brand-shakes-up-rivals-wsj

FOUR Marketers Lie, but Numbers Don't

Seth Godin, *All Marketers Are Liars: The Power of Telling Authentic Stories in a Low-Trust World*, 2005.

Georgia Institute of Technology MGT6308EM Strategic Brand Management MBA class, *Warby Parker Brand Consulting Project*, by students Braddon Calloway, Steven Carriere, Robin Jenkins, Bethany Schuster, and Julia Snell, Summer 2018.

FIVE Opportunity from Chaos

Sun Tzu, *The Art of War*, circa 500 BC.

The Washington Post, *The mind-blowing science of how Febreze hides your smelliness*, August 17, 2015 by Rachel Feltman; https://www.washingtonpost.com/news/speaking-of-science/wp/2015/08/17/the-mind-blowing-science-of-how-febreze-hides-your-smelliness/?utm_term=.7ff8fd654bbe

Keller, K. L. Strategic, *Brand Management: Building, Measuring, and Managing Brand Equity*, 4th Edition, Prentice Hall Publishers, ISBN-10: 0132664259, 2012.

Written by Design, *The ABCs of Good Concept Writing*, March 15, 2017 by Patti Purcell; http://writingbydesignllc.com/2017/03/the-abcs-of-good-concept-writing

Business Insider, *This spray that can replace your iron is a lifesaver for the business traveler*, March 7, 2016 by Dennis Green; https://www.businessinsider.com/best-ironing-alternative-2016-3

Pantene Up to 10X Stronger Hair print advertisement is used for educational purposes under the Fair Use copyright doctrine. Copyright Disclaimer under section 107 of the Copyright Act of 1976, allowance is made for "fair use" for purposes such as criticism, comment, news reporting, teaching, scholarship, education and research. Fair use is a use permitted by copyright statute that might otherwise be infringing.

SIX Sell a Little, Learn a Lot

ArchPoint, *Wielded Properly, ArchPoint's OGSM Process aligns every element of your business—and improves execution*; https://archpointgroup.com/consulting/#strategyogsm

Leighton Broadcasting, *Clicks, Impressions, and Conversions, Oh My! Digital Marketing Terms you Need to Know*, April 4, 2016 by Stephanie Theisen; http://blog.leightonbroadcasting.com/blog/clicks-impressions-and-conversions-oh-my-digital-marketing-terms-you-need-to-know

Georgia Institute of Technology MGT4304A Strategic Brand Management undergraduate class, *Urban Tree Cidery Brand Analysis Project*, Fall 2016 by students Jake Anderson, Connor Durkin, William Kittle, and Donovan Shuman.

Georgia Institute of Technology MGT4910D Independent Study, *Testing the Mgt4304, Urban Tree Cidery Brand Analysis Project Recommendation in a Real World Setting*, Fall 2017 by student Connor Durkin.

Urban Tree Cidery, From Grove to Glass internet banner advertisement is used for educational purposes under the Fair Use copyright doctrine. Copyright Disclaimer under section 107 of the Copyright Act of 1976, allowance is made for "fair use" for purposes such as criticism, comment, news reporting, teaching, scholarship, education and research. Fair use is a use permitted by copyright statute that might otherwise be infringing.

Urban Tree Cidery, A Unique Taste of Atlanta student led internet banner advertisement is used for educational purposes under the Fair Use copyright doctrine. Copyright Disclaimer under section 107 of the Copyright Act of 1976, allowance is made for "fair use" for purposes such as criticism, comment, news reporting, teaching, scholarship, education and research. Fair use is a use permitted by copyright statute that might otherwise be infringing.

SEVEN First Moment of Truth

A. G. Lafley, *First Moment of Truth* dialogue at the Procter & Gamble Company, circa 2000.

Harvard Business Review, *What Only the CEO Can Do*, May 2009 by A. G. Lafley; https://hbr.org/2009/05/what-only-the-ceo-can-do

Advertising Age, *Folgers' New Instant Shoots from the Hip; P&G's Coffee Brand Aims Ads Younger, Tests Café Latte Line*, November 15, 1999 by Louise Kramer; https://adage.com/print/60314

Folgers Café Latte packaging and *Folgers Cappuccino* packaging demonstrations are used for educational purposes under the Fair Use copyright doctrine. Copyright Disclaimer under section 107 of the Copyright Act of 1976, allowance is made for "fair use" for purposes such as criticism, comment, news reporting, teaching, scholarship, education and research. Fair use is a use permitted by copyright statute that might otherwise be infringing.

Shopper Marketing Magazine, *P&G Focuses on Winning with Brands at Retail*, January 18, 2016 by Suzy Frisch; https://shoppermarketingmag.com/pg-focuses-winning-brands-retail

Harvard Business Review, *The Elements of Value*, September 2016 by Eric Almquist, John Senior, and Nicolas Bloch;

https://hbr.org/2016/09/the-elements-of-value

Brand Packaging Magazine, *It's Time for Brands to Go Back to the Drawing Board: Design is failing, creating waste. Revisit and revise your strategy for a successful, sustainable brand,* April 11, 2016 by Laura Zielinski; https://www.brandpackaging.com/articles/85316-its-time-for-brands-to-go-back-to-the-drawing-board

Adweek, *'Product Experience' Drives Performance,* November 5, 2007 by Noreen O'Leary; https://www.adweek.com/brand-marketing/product-experience-drives-performance-90914/

Colgate-Palmolive press release, *Introducing New Colgate Simply White® Whitening Toothpaste,* October 15, 2003; https://investor.colgatepalmolive.com/news-releases/news-release-details/introducing-new-colgate-simply-whiter-whitening-toothpaste right statute that might otherwise be infringing.

CNN Money, *Product packaging that pays: How consumer-product companies are revamping their containers to jump-start sales*, October 9, 2006 by Susanna Hamner; https://money.cnn.com/2006/07/06/technology/packagingthatpays.biz2/index.htm

EIGHT Product Placebo

Wall Street Journal, *Why Placebos Really Work: The Latest Science, New evidence suggests the fake drugs may cause changes in the body, not just the mind,* July 18, 2016 by Sumathi Reddy; https://www.wsj.com/articles/why-placebos-really-work-the-latest-science-1468863413

FDA Guidance for Institutional Review Boards and Clinical Investigators, July 12, 2018; https://www.fda.gov/RegulatoryInformation/Guidances/ucm126501.htm

Harvard Health Publishing, *A placebo can work even when you know it's a placebo*, July 7, 2016 by Mallika Marshall, MD; https://www.health.harvard.edu/blog/placebo-can-work-even-know-placebo-201607079926

The New England Journal of Medicine, *A Controlled Trial of Arthroscopic Surgery for Osteoarthritis of the Knee*, July 11, 2002 by J. Bruce Moseley, M.D., Kimberly O'Malley, Ph.D., Nancy J. Petersen, Ph.D., Terri J. Menke, Ph.D., Baruch A. Brody, Ph.D., David H. Kuykendall, Ph.D., John C. Hollingsworth, Dr.P.H., Carol M. Ashton, M.D., M.P.H., and Nelda P. Wray, M.D., M.P.H.. N Engl J Med 2002;347:81-88
DOI: 10.1056/NEJMoa013259; https://www.nejm.org/doi/full/10.1056/NEJMoa013259

Ad Age, *P&G Shifts Strategy for Dryel*, January 24, 2000 by Jack Neff; https://adage.com/article/news/p-g-shifts-strategy-dryel/59687/

Psychology Today, A Creativity Lesson From Betty Crocker,

January 19, 2014 by Drew Boyd; https://www.psychology-today.com/us/blog/inside-the-box/201401/creativity-lesson-betty-crocker

The New York Times, *When Flour Power Invaded the Kitchen*, April 14, 2004 by Dinitia Smith; https://www.nytimes.com/2004/04/14/dining/when-flour-power-invaded-the-kitchen.html

Ad Age, *U by Kotex*, November 15, 2010 by Jack Neff; https://adage.com/article/print-edition/u-kotex-america-s-hottest-brands-2010/147067

Cara Chiarello, former Creative Director at the oneCARE Company, designed and modeled in the upgraded *Dryel* package. Chiarello designed the jeans and sweater *Dryel* print advertisements.

Levinson W, Roter DL, Mullooly JP, Dull VT, Frankel RM. *Physician-Patient Communication: The Relationship With Malpractice Claims Among Primary Care Physicians and Surgeons. JAMA.* 1997;277(7):553–559. doi:10.1001/jama.1997.03540310051034; https://jamanetwork.com/journals/jama/article-abstract/414233?redirect=true

EPILOGUE 64/4 Brand

Adweek, *How a German-Jewish Mystic Created an American Soap Company Determined to Clean Up the Planet: The unusual story behind Dr. Bronner's suds,* March 14, 2017 by Robert Klara; https://www.adweek.com/brand-marketing/how-dr-bronners-is-taking-over-soap-dishes-across-america

Simply Psychology, *Type A and B personality,* 2017 by Saul McLeod; https://www.simplypsychology.org/personality-a.html

Management Today, *UK: The dawn of a cultural revolution. - Breakthrough is the key word at P&G. But can it break through to a more open management culture?* published March 1, 1998 and updated August 31, 2010 by Alan Mitchell; https://www.managementtoday.co.uk/uk-dawn-cultural-revolution/article/411605

ABOUT THE AUTHOR

The 80/20 of Coaching

AARON HACKETT has been at the Georgia Institute of Technology's Scheller College of Business since 2013, where he teaches the Strategic Brand Management courses for MBA and undergraduate students. In addition to teaching, Aaron consults with brands and leads brand training through his 80/20 Brand consulting firm.

Aaron is a marketing leader with experience in both Fortune 500 and emerging organizations. Beginning his marketing career at The Procter & Gamble Company as an assistant brand manager and later progressing to vice president of marketing and general manager at The oneCARE Company, Aaron has helped leading organizations launch successful new product initiatives, fix under-performing brands, and leverage digital marketing to efficiently build revenue.

Aaron has delivered successful product innovations such as *Folgers* ground flavored coffee and *Healthy Choice's* Asian steamed meals, resulting in first-year revenues of $10MM and $23MM respectively. He has managed business unit brand portfolios, such as The oneCARE Company's $60MM fabric care business unit featuring *Dryel*, and several P&G licensed brands. Aaron has balanced his line management success with corporate mastery experience that allowed him to deliver P&G's approach for in-store messaging.

Aaron is an MBA graduate of Stanford University. He received his M.S. in Industrial Engineering from the University of Tennessee at Knoxville and B.S. in Mechanical Engineering from the University of Texas at Austin. Before marketing, Aaron worked several years as an engineer and information technology professional at Bechtel National, Incorporated. He lives in the Atlanta area with his wife and three children.

To connect with Aaron about training or consulting, email 80/20 Brand at connect@8020brand.com.

Made in the USA
Columbia, SC
10 June 2020